The JEWISH BOOK *of* GRIEF & HEALING

A Spiritual Companion for Mourning

EDITED BY STUART M. MATLINS
AND THE EDITORS AT JEWISH LIGHTS

Preface by Rabbi Anne Brener, LCSW
author of *Mourning & Mitzvah: A Guided Journal for Walking
the Mourner's Path through Grief to Healing*

Foreword by Dr. Ron Wolfson
author of *A Time to Mourn, a Time to Comfort: A Guide to Jewish Bereavement*

For People of All Faiths, All Backgrounds
JEWISH LIGHTS Publishing

The Jewish Book of Grief & Healing:
A Spiritual Companion for Mourning

2016 Quality Paperback Edition
© 2016 by Jewish Lights Publishing
Preface © 2016 by Anne Brener
Foreword © 2016 by Ron Wolfson

Library of Congress Cataloging-in-Publication Data
Names: Matlins, Stuart M., editor. | Wolfson, Ron, The work of mourning.
    Container of (work) :
Title: The Jewish book of grief and healing : a spiritual companion for mourning the loss of a loved one / edited by Stuart M. Matlins and the editors at Jewish Lights ; preface by Rabbi Anne Brener, LCSW ; foreword by Dr. Ron Wolfson.
Description: Woodstock, VT : Jewish Lights Publishing, a division of LongHill Partners, Inc., [2016] | Includes bibliographical references and index.
Identifiers: LCCN 2015050759| ISBN 9781580238526 (pbk.) | ISBN 9781580238618 (ebook)
Subjects: LCSH: Jewish mourning customs. | Consolation (Judaism)
Classification: LCC BM712 .J49 2016 | DDC 296.4/45—dc23 LC record available at http://lccn.loc.gov/2015050759

Manufactured in the United States of America
Cover design: Jenny Buono
Cover art: © Capture Light / Shutterstock
Interior design: Tim Holtz

For People of All Faiths, All Backgrounds
Jewish Lights Publishing
A Division of LongHill Partners, Inc.
An Imprint of Turner Publishing Company
4507 Charlotte Avenue, Suite 100
Nashville, TN 37209
Tel: (615) 255-2665
www.jewishlights.com

Contents

Preface

Rabbi Anne Brener, LCSW

Mourning is not simply adjusting to the loss of someone or something central to our lives. It is also a profound encounter with what it means to be human, as well as what is holy in the face of the reality of death.

Many of you may experience mourning as an earthquake that buckles the ground beneath your feet, shattering your assumptions about the world you inhabited before grief struck. In addition to the needs to turn your physical connection with the person who died into a spiritual one—continuing the conversation that seemingly ended with the loss—and to resolve unfinished issues, grief can raise questions about justice, mortality, God, and the afterlife. With proper guidance, these questions provide initiation into the fact of mortality, helping you to reclaim your connection with who or what has been lost, to make peace with a world in which living things (and those we love) die, and to forge a new relationship with God.

Mourning can open doors you may not have imagined before your life was shaken by loss. This book provides keys to those doors and a way into the rooms beyond them. Whether you stand at grief's threshold or give counsel to someone who does, this book can offer guidance.

As each door opens, it issues an invitation into one of the essential conversations that will enable the birth of a new vision of yourself, allowing you to thrive in a changed world. While this possibility is beyond imagination at the onset of grief, it is real. Healing comes from a mysterious place. It will come, if you are willing to surrender your assumptions and be curious about the unknown: the unknown rooms beyond the doors that these existential conversations open to you.

This collection gathers treasures from the books that Jewish Lights Publishing has brought us in the last quarter century. It assembles a community of wise and caring authors, each of whom has gone beyond the threshold to wrestle with the challenging questions that grief calls forth. With words of wisdom, ranging from comforting to provocative, each author stands at the entrance to one of mourning's doors, extending a hand to offer the key you will need, inviting you into one of these deep conversations.

When Jewish Lights began, in the last decade of the last century, it promised to deepen the Jewish conversation by "publishing books that reflect the Jewish wisdom tradition for people of all faiths, all backgrounds." Speaking in a language accessible across the spectrum of Jewish life and beyond its borders, these books have shepherded in a new paradigm for Jewish thought and experience, which is, in fact, anything but new.

The focus of Jewish Lights on Judaism as a path of spirituality and healing restores an ancient vision of the faith. This vision is articulated in Psalm 90, in words attributed to King David and said to be written for the dedication of the Jerusalem Temple. I believe that these words reveal an intention that the Temple be a place for healing: "You have turned my mourning into dancing."

This book helps to choreograph that "dance." It accompanies mourners and their supporters through grief's often painful twists and turns, in the dance of healing facilitated through the Jewish mourning rituals. I welcome you to the Jewish Lights community. I am confident that you will find companionship in these pages.

Foreword

Dr. Ron Wolfson

Grieving the dead is one of the most challenging experiences of being alive. It is a process that engulfs the whole of us—our minds, our hearts, even our bodies. Grief sweeps over us like waves crashing on the beach, threatening to drown us in salty tears of mourning and loss. Yet Judaism provides a wise path on the road to healing.

When my mother, Bernice Paperny Wolfson, died, I thought I was ready. I had written a book about mourning and comforting, taught a university course on the subject, and offered lectures and workshops for the bereaved. And then I learned a powerful lesson about life: nothing adequately prepares you for confronting the reality of death.

The phone call came from my brother Doug. "Mom is in the hospital. She's in a delirium." My wife, Susie, and I were at a wedding in Indiana. We immediately flew to Omaha and rushed to Mom's bedside. To calm her from her delirium, the doctors had induced her into a coma. Tests were taken. Shadows appeared on the scans, indicative of tumors. Much later, we would learn that Mom had refused all screening for cancer. If she had it, she didn't want to know. After a few days, she awoke and we had almost a week with her. On the Monday she was scheduled to transfer to the Hospice House, she died, peacefully.

Quickly, that very afternoon, we gathered with the rabbi, wrote an obituary, and made the arrangements with the *chevra kadisha* and the cemetery. We set up the meal of condolence. Word spread quickly that the funeral was the next day.

As we pulled into Beth El Cemetery for the graveside service, I thought I was ready. I knew the prescribed rituals. I anticipated the thud of dirt on the casket. I was sixty years old, but from the minute the coffin was placed in front of me, I cried like a baby. Not a few quiet sobs. Completely, unexpectedly, I was overwhelmed by an uncontrollable, sustained wail of tears for Mom. The service was meaningful, the words of the *kaddish* resonated, and the crowd of family and friends offered comfort. I thought the worst of it was over as the *shiva* period began.

But that night, as I lay restless in bed, the grief suddenly took on a physical dimension. I had heard of, indeed written about, this manifestation, but now it was settling in my lower back, as if I had torn a muscle. Soon, the pain spread throughout my body. It was difficult to fall asleep, my mind racing with memories and stories and images of Mom. I thought I was ready ... but I was not.

As you will read in the pages of this important and insightful resource, there is no timeline for grief. Yes, Jewish tradition wisely delineates the calendar for mourning—the seven days of *shiva*, the first thirty days, the first year, the *yartzeit* anniversary, the four occasions of reciting the *Yizkor* prayers on the holidays of Yom Kippur, Sukkot, Passover, and Shavuot. But no one can predict how you will grieve ... or for that matter, heal. Each of us will experience this process uniquely.

Judaism offers another message of comfort: you are not alone. When you are connected to family, friends, and community, they provide physical, psychological, and social support. The Hebrew word for "funeral" is *levaya*— "to accompany." In this extraordinary volume, Stuart M. Matlins and his colleagues at Jewish Lights have brilliantly collected words of wisdom from many of the best teachers of our time to accompany you on this journey. May these words help guide you along this path and may God comfort you among all the mourners of Zion and Jerusalem.

Jewish Mourning

Grieving is the way we mend broken hearts.... The process of mourning is the way the psyche, bruised and battered by the pain of loss, heals itself.

Dr. Ron Wolfson

Grief is not only a psychological response to a mystery. It is part of the mystery itself. Mourning is an essential *process* of *tikkun* (repair) by which the world can continue to function.

Rabbi Margaret Holub

No one is prepared for grief. Even if you have been anticipating a loss, you will discover that there is no such thing as "anticipatory grieving." No words on a page can ultimately make sense of it all for you. But for those moments when you long for someone to at least attempt to explain what is happening around you, Rabbi Margaret Holub and Dr. Ron Wolfson offer a compassionate overview of the practices and rituals Judaism provides for mourners, including a range of traditional observances not typically made use of in less-traditional communities.

1

You will likely find these practices and insights helpful in guiding you through your grief. But sometimes the ancient words may feel less comforting than you'd like. Rabbi Kerry Olitzky admits how difficult it is to bless the "True Judge" for the cause of our grief, but reminds us that the True Judge is also a Rock for support and strength. Other contributors share thoughtful perspectives about the afterlife and the end of time, and questions to help you be aware of the expectations you have about what mourning ought to look like.

Modern Western culture often seeks to ignore death, to gloss over grief, to get back to regular life as soon as possible. Let the ancient wisdom of Judaism guide you, wrap you in the comfort of healing rituals and community, and help you walk the mourner's path from grief to healing.

Mourning Rituals

Rabbi Margaret Holub

"I've been with many people whose grief has been beyond bearing. And in some ways it has been the best thing that ever happened to them,"[1] writes Stephen Levine in a popular book that I turned to when I was in mourning. People flock to Levine's seminars—people with cancer, people who have lost children, people who are reckoning with death. He, Elisabeth Kübler-Ross, and others have brought death front and center on the American stage.[2]

When the man I loved died, I read Levine and Kübler-Ross and gratefully accepted their adjurations not to stifle my grief, to welcome and feel fully each of its inevitable stages. I wept every day for two years. This new psychological perspective on grief probably saved my life, and I am thankful that a "stiff upper lip" is no longer considered a virtue. But for all my willingness to face and express my feelings, something was missing for me at the time of my grieving. I needed a deeper understanding of death and of my own heartbreak.

Grief is not only a psychological response to a mystery. It is part of the mystery itself. Mourning is an essential process of *tikkun* (repair) by which the world can continue to function. Jewish tradition is rich in ritual that helps people survive the death of a loved one. And this ritual is grounded in a particular cosmology, without which the ritual may be comforting, but does not make philosophical sense....

Excerpted from the award-winning *Lifecycles*, Volume 1: *Jewish Women on Life Passages and Personal Milestones* (Jewish Lights), edited by Rabbi Debra Orenstein. **Rabbi Margaret Holub** is the spiritual leader of a rural alternative shtetl on the North Coast of California.

The Metaphysics of Mourning

How can we tell where one person ends and another begins? The material finitude of our bodies is evident, but the borders of the soul are less definite. We merge as we learn from one another, live together and accrue common experiences, take on each other's projects, and enter into shared fates. Love blurs the boundaries between one soul and another. In fact, love might be defined as that very erosion, absorption, commingling.

When the tenuous coupling of a person's body and soul is undone by death, the bond of body and soul within each person who has been close to the *met/metah* [the deceased] is also weakened. The breath of God within all who were bound up with that person wishes, as it were, to leave the bodies of its temporary residence and to flee to the one great Source. And so it is that a survivor must mourn, to heal and repair the bond between his or her own body and soul—literally, in some measure, to stay alive.

Anthropologist Victor Turner speaks of liminality, of a time when everything is changing, when a person is especially vulnerable, almost as though his or her skin were missing. At such a time, Turner says, the community comes together, the tradition steps in, and together we walk the person through the tunnel of liminality to a new place in a world reconnected.[3]

Mourning is perhaps the ultimate liminal, or disconnected, state. Outside us, the web of life has been torn. Within us, body and soul are wrestling apart. Our tradition recognizes that, while body and soul may have been severed almost instantaneously for the loved one who died, the reweaving of body and soul in the survivors—the agenda of mourning—happens in stages over weeks, months, years, and generations. No wonder, then, that the reuniting of the bodies and souls of all people for the great messianic resurrection is imagined to require millennia of preparation.

A Few Holy Tools

The task of mourning is to re-cement the bond between body and soul in people facing the internal rift left by the death of their loved one. Jewish tradition offers a set of finely crafted tools for reviving the union that makes for life in survivors. These rituals have a metaphysical as well as a psychological dimension.[4]

As a rabbi with a non-halakhic [nontraditional] orientation, who considers Jewish law instructive rather than binding, I often find myself in the ironic position of—for want of a better word—negotiating with mourners to observe traditional mourning rituals: "Maybe you would consider three days of *shiva* (formal period of mourning, usually seven days) and a minyan (prayer quorum) on the thirtieth day after the death? No? How about just one minyan to say *kaddish* (mourner's prayer) and, later, an unveiling?" In almost every other aspect of Jewish practice, I think that people should do what they want to do, what coheres with their vision of life. But I sense that the task of mourning may demand something different than what people want in the moment, may in fact be exactly the opposite of what they want. And there may be more at stake than they can possibly know in those early days of grief.

Below are a few examples of Jewish mourning practices[5] and the cosmological concerns that I believe they address:

Aninut (Period Between Death and Burial)

Jewish law exempts *kerovim* (close relatives obligated to mourn) from normal religious requirements during the period between the death and the burial of their beloved. The usual reason given is that *onenim* (the bereft during *aninut*) are engaged in one commandment—i.e., preparing for the funeral—and are therefore exempt from others (*Shulhan Arukh Yoreh De'ah* 341:1). However, we can also read the *halakhah* [traditional Jewish law] according to a cosmological construct. *Onenim* are exempt, from this point of view, because only the fully living must perform *mitzvot* (commandments), and, following the death of a beloved, survivors border on death themselves. This cosmological perspective is reinforced by the striking, halakhic exemption of the community from caring for mourners in those first hours or days. The community is not expected to visit, bring food, or even extend words of comfort. It is as though the angel of death were still in the house, stalking with sword raised. Until the burial, the death is still happening, body and soul are shaking apart throughout the household. The community stays away, as rebuilding cannot begin until the earthquake is over.

I well remember a moment, immediately after the death of the man I loved, when I was at the home of friends. It was a gray afternoon, and I sat outside on a log, weeping. As I sat there, it began to rain. And I recall vividly that, at that moment, the decision to stand up and walk into the house was simply beyond me, and I sat outside until I was soaked. Right then I was like a *metah*, unable to carry on even the simplest functions of life. It was too soon to comfort me, too soon to feed me, too soon to reason with me.

During the time of *aninut*, the *kerovim* are not traditionally involved with caring for the dead body, which has its own needs. This work is done by others, either at a funeral home or, more traditionally, by a *hevrah kaddishah* (burial society). Members of the burial society wash and dress the body and accompany it until the moment of burial. When our community's *hevrah kaddishah* arrives to do its holy work, a family member or close friend of the one who died will sometimes ask to help. We discourage it, but once or twice relatives of the deceased have joined in. It takes great strength of soul, and a certain amount of bodily strength as well, to do *levayat hamet* (caring for/accompanying the dead). Close family and friends, we have learned, are invariably too broken to do this work. At the moment when death is so fresh, when it may still be invisibly in process, the work of the *kerovim* is to survive.

Hespedim (Eulogies)

At the funeral at least one eulogy is usually given. In my community, often everyone present will offer a memory, teaching, or observation about the person who has died. And these narratives fix, like fixer in a darkroom, an image of the life which blew through the universe like a comet.

We have all had the experience of coming home after a vacation. Someone asks us, "How was your trip?" And to answer, we condense days or weeks into a narrative. After we have told a few people about our vacation, we may notice that the actual memory of the trip begins to fade. What remains is the story we have been telling. So, too, at the moment when we bury the body, when we pray for the ascension of the soul, we hold on to the story.

Kevurah (Burial)

People who attend a Jewish funeral for the first time often remark on the beautiful, brutal custom of having family members pitch shovelsful of dirt into the grave. "It makes death real," they say. What resounds in my recollection of burials is the sound of clods of soil hitting the wooden coffin, the hollow thud. This is something you would never do to any living being, much less to a person you loved. And so it hits you as you hold the shovel: Whatever is in that hole in the ground is not that person. Their existence is over; body and soul are wholly separated. Any ambivalence, lingering question, or hope ends with that hollow sound.

Kaddish (Mourner's Prayer)

Rabbi Billy Berkowitz conceived the exercise of giving his congregants a prayer book and a red pencil and challenging them to edit out anything they found to be untrue. I asked Billy what, if anything, he would retain. "Only a fragment of one line," he said, "from the *kaddish*: '[God is] far beyond any blessings, songs, praises, and consolations that can be expressed in the world.'"

There are many forms of the *kaddish* recited in prayer services and study halls, but mourners stand and recite a special *kaddish*. Their *kaddish* echoes what appears eminently true for mourners, that God is far away, "far beyond," that the words of most prayers may not even come close to the feelings in the speaker's heart. We tend to think of the *kaddish* as a brave or comforting affirmation of God's glory, but from the perspective of the mourner, it may just as well be an acknowledgment of God's apparent distance.

Reintroducing Festivity Gradually

For the first seven days following the funeral, body and soul are minimally tended. Most conspicuously, any element of the erotic, of the life force, is muted. One does not have sex (Babylonian Talmud, *Mo'ed Katan* 21a; *Shulhan Arukh Yoreh De'ah* 383:1). Mourners do not even wash or dress attractively (*Shulhan Arukh Yoreh De'ah* 389:1; Babylonian Talmud, *Mo'ed Katan* 17b; *Sede Hemed, Avelut* 40). Sitting at normal height, wearing leather, shaving (for men), and wearing shoes are likewise prohibited (*Shulhan Arukh Yoreh De'ah* 387:1–2, 380:1, 382:1, 390:1), and it is customary not to look in the mirror.

After seven days (sometimes fewer if the death happens shortly before a festival) mourners clean up, dress in fresh clothing, and go back to work. But festivity is not permitted for three more weeks, or for a full year if it is a parent who died (Shah on *Shulhan Arukh Yoreh De'ah* 344:9). While it is permitted to attend lifecycle rituals, the festivities afterward are to be avoided. Festivity is the linking of body and soul. While their bond is fragile, one does not stretch it by trying to be merry.

Finally, after thirty days or one year has ended, one may again dance, listen to music, attend parties, throw oneself into the happiness of the community. The *tikkun* is thereby considered to be more or less complete.

Elleh Ezkerah (These Do I Remember): Ongoing Markers

One never finishes mourning. Body and soul are rejoined, but with a scar at the bond. And so it is that two sorts of ritual mourning continue for the life of the mourner. On anniversaries of the death, the mourners are singled out. They light a *yartzeit* candle (candle burned on the anniversary of a family member's death) and stand in the congregation to say *kaddish*. In addition, four times a year there is a moment of collective mourning. The *Yizkor* (memorial service) is essentially identical to the funeral service for an individual, but here the names of all the loved ones of the entire community are read and/or recorded. Everyone mourns together, publicly. How different it is to mark the *yartzeit* of a family member than it is to memorialize all the deaths in a community. The former custom makes a private, cosmological point: You, and not your loved one, are alive to stand and stand out, in the community. The latter makes a communal point about shared destiny; everyone sustains loss and everyone is part of the community of comforters. In many synagogues, these ideas are physicalized in the choreography of the prayer services: Only those who are in mourning or observing a *yartzeit* stand when the *kaddish* is said, but the entire community stands during *Yizkor*....

To What End?

There is no teacher like mourning. Now that death has come close to me, both by taking the man I once loved and then by almost taking me, I am not the person I was before. I can only describe the change in the most personal terms. I am so glad to be alive, so grateful that my parents are alive and healthy, so thankful that I went on to love another man and make such an interesting and enjoyable life with him. I am richly blessed to live in a loving community in a beautiful place.

Yet, it could all go in a minute. It *will* all go in a minute. This life is a brief stop, whether I die tomorrow or in fifty years. I would love not to know this, to have the innocent certainty that, when loved ones set out on a journey, they will return unharmed, that I can go out to sea in my boat, play in the waves, and not be swallowed up. But I am more grateful now than I ever was in my innocence.

In the end it is all a gift, is it not? The brief entwinement of body and soul, the breath of God that gives and sustains human life, creates such a colorful, sparkling trail as it arcs through time. It is so ephemeral, and yet it affects everything. As we say when we open our eyes every morning: "I give thanks to You, God of life who is eternal, for returning my soul to me this morning. Great is Your faithfulness."

The Work of Mourning

Dr. Ron Wolfson

Grieving is the way we mend broken hearts. When we sustain a bad wound, the body heals in stages: Initially, we feel shock and numbness, then the sharp pain of the injury, and slowly the hurt subsides. Even so, we are often left with a scar, reminding us of the seriousness of the trauma. "Grief-work," the process of mourning, is the way the psyche, bruised and battered by the pain of loss, heals itself.

Responses to loss cannot be accurately predicted nor explained in neatly defined phases. Just as in the process of dying, bereavement involves a number of responses that come in and out of the mind and body at different times. In unexpected moments, just when we think the acute pain is over, a wave of sorrow or a deep ache of loss can overcome us.

Moreover, there is no timeline for the healing of grief. For some, the intensity of pain subsides within months; for others, it is years before the adjustment to the loss is in place. It is critically important for mourners to realize that there is no "right" way to grieve, nor is there any "limit" on how long the "phases" of grief will last. Each of us will experience bereavement in a unique way....

When the numbness and shock wear off, the reality of the loss hits. Intense emotions often boil over in fits of sadness, anger, melancholy, and anguish. When grief reaches the heart, the real pain begins.

In the Jewish tradition, grief reaches the heart at the funeral. Everything about the funeral is designed to confront the bereaved with the reality of

Excerpted from *A Time to Mourn, a Time to Comfort,* 2nd Edition: *A Guide to Jewish Bereavement* (Jewish Lights) by **Dr. Ron Wolfson**, a beloved and popular speaker on Judaism and Jewish life and Fingerhut Professor of Education at American Jewish University in Los Angeles. Dr. Wolfson's other books include *Relational Judaism: Using the Power of Relationships to Transform the Jewish Community* and *The Seven Questions You're Asked in Heaven: Reviewing & Renewing Your Life on Earth* (both Jewish Lights).

death. The eulogy stimulates our memories and our emotions, the prayers talk not just of the demise of the deceased, but of the mortality of all human beings and the confrontation with the grave. The thud of the earth on the casket shakes the bereaved out of shock and disbelief, clearing the way for the difficult work of mourning.

Aveilut, mourning, begins at this moment of raw emotion. The *shiva* time that lies ahead will be filled with the symptoms of grief-work. Among them are:

Sadness

The sadness that the bereaved experience is overwhelming. It is an ache felt in the deepest part of the soul. It is a feeling of complete emptiness, hollowness. Its most predominant expression is tears—tears of sadness, tears of loss. While there are predictable times when the tears flow, there are also unexpected moments that trigger them. Suddenly, a memory pops into your head, and you begin sobbing. Seeing someone with whom you and the deceased shared wonderful times will bring on uncontrollable weeping. You open a closet door after the funeral, and at the first glance of a row of suits, you break down. Eventually, you cry yourself out, exhausted. Of course, it is impossible to enjoy yourself with amusements, parties, television. It is even difficult to enjoy the company of those who give you the most pleasure—children, grandchildren, friends. Sometimes a feeling of despair comes with the tears. But, often, the tears ultimately bring a kind of comfort, the lubricating fluid of the healing process.

The Bible is filled with accounts of the wailing that accompanies loss. Jewish tradition allows for the sadness of bereavement, encouraging its expression throughout the funeral and *shiva* period.

Anger

A natural response to loss is anger—anger born of frustration and helplessness. This anger is directed at many—doctors, hospitals, drunken drivers, rabbis, employers, family, friends—even God. It is not uncommon to find yourself lashing out at those you love the most.

Why my son? Why my wife? Why has this bad thing happened to this good person? From Abraham to Job to Wiesel to Kushner, the questioning of God is well within the mainstream of the Jewish response to loss.

Guilt

Guilt is one of the most common responses to loss. It appears in a variety of ways:

- Guilt born of survival. "I should have gone first."
- Guilt born of anger. "Why did you die and leave me?"
- Guilt born of the inability to cope with loss. "I shouldn't be so distraught. Why can't I get ahold of myself?"
- Guilt born of feeling relief that the deceased is gone. "How dare I feel happy again!"
- Guilt born of regret. "If only I had taken her to another doctor …" "I should never have driven him so hard …" "I'll never forgive myself for the fight we had …"

Pangs of guilt are natural and, according to some experts, necessary. In a twist of irony, guilt feelings, when overcome, enable the mourner to consider the positive ways he or she acted. "Yes, I could have done more for Mom, but now that I think about it, I really was a pretty good son." Of course, overwhelming guilt can be disabling and should be dealt with appropriately. Ultimately, whatever guilt feelings exist should be forgiven. Forgiving oneself is an important step on the road to healing grief.

Jewish tradition knew this. In a practice that unfortunately is no longer in vogue, it suggested that each person at a funeral ask the deceased for forgiveness. Surely the rabbis knew that it was unlikely the deceased would hear this plea (although many of them had a vivid imagination of the afterlife). Rather, the psychological wisdom of asking forgiveness lies in the expiation of guilt that accompanies the plea. We ask not that the deceased forgive us; we ask ourselves for forgiveness—a task that is far more difficult. Judaism wants us not to be too hard on ourselves.

Physical Complaints

Mourners often complain of physical ailments, including shortness of breath, tightness in the throat, feelings of emptiness in the stomach, overwhelming weakness, headaches. Most bereaved have very little appetite, experience difficulty sleeping, and feel totally exhausted.

Judaism insists that the bereaved eat immediately after the funeral as a sign of the slow return to normalcy, yet most mourners report difficulty in consuming this meal. During the course of the *shiva*, this feeling subsides and appetite returns. However, the intensity of the *shiva* often leads to a lack of sleep and a profound sense of exhaustion. In fact, the feeling of exhaustion is the most frequently cited response to the *shiva* experience.

Fear

Having stared death in the face, the bereaved often express their own fear of dying or of other loved ones dying. Or widows fear being alone, children fear losing the other parent, and adult children fear the future once both parents are gone.

Jewish tradition attempts to smother these fears by surrounding the bereaved with community. The message is clear: "You are not alone." That is why the community comes to the mourner for the *shiva*, that is why the community welcomes the bereaved back to its fold on the Shabbat during *shiva*, that is why each experience of Jewish mourning is celebrated not alone, but within the context of a supportive community.

Pining and Searching

Pining is the soulful longing for the deceased that leads to searching, the powerful urge to find a "lost" love. Often, this phenomenon is uncanny and disconcerting. You begin to "see" your loved one in the faces of others. You "hear" his or her voice. You sense the presence of the deceased in a room, at a table, during a prayer.

Judaism wants us never to forget the memory of the departed. The *shiva* is not the end of mourning—it is just the beginning. We mourn the loss of loved ones four times a year during the *Yizkor* memorial service and on every anniversary of a death for the rest of our lives. Jewish tradition teaches us that we can never get them back physically, but we can have them with us in our memories forever.

Lapses in Clear Thinking

The bereaved may experience enormous emotional swings that sometimes result in such a mental tumult that normally clear-thinking people can become confused, use poor judgment, and even experience temporary memory loss. The days immediately following the funeral are not a good time to make important decisions and choices.

Again, the wisdom of the seven-day *shiva* period allows the bereaved time to gather themselves for the inevitable decision making that follows a loss.

"Where shall Mom live?" "What about the will?" "How do we divide up the personal items in the household?" When a family sits *shiva* for seven days, there is time for the initial grief to subside so these decisions can be made.

Falling Apart

Mourners often evidence changes of behavior in both relationships with others and in daily activities. For those who grieve, the simplest of chores—paying bills, shopping for groceries—often feel like major burdens. Sometimes the mourner wanders around the house, aimlessly picking up things, putting them down, rearranging photos on mantles, or simply staring into space. The mourner loses control of his eating or drinking, takes foolish risks, gives away precious possessions. The mourner feels like she's falling apart.

Judaism suggests the mourner spend thirty days slowly returning to regular routines, to work, and to the daily challenges of living. For thirty days after the funeral, the bereaved's activities are restricted somewhat, allowing a gradual return to the complexities of living. During this time, friends and family can provide tremendous comfort in reassuring the bereaved that these feelings of being out of control are perfectly normal for those who have experienced profound loss. For some, a support group can be helpful in smoothing the transition back to normalcy. The important message is that these feelings will subside in time. Grief-work is not over quickly.

How Am I Supposed to Feel?

Rabbi Anne Brener, LCSW

Before we "cover the mirrors" to begin the mourning journey, there are a few things about yourself that we need to look at…. Remember that mourning is not only a memorial to the person whom you have lost. It is also a testimonial to the process by which you summon—and strengthen—your own inner resources…. Please remember that mourning includes obligations to *yourself* as well as to the person you have lost.

Finding Healthy Models for Your Mourning Process

Properly confronting your grief is not self-indulgence. It is sound preventive medicine. The saying by Dr. Henry Maudsley, an eighteenth-century British psychiatrist, "A sorrow that has no vent in tears makes other organs weep," underscores the importance of mourning.

Often, after the death of someone close, people have irrational fears concerning their health. In fact, physical symptoms often accompany grief. These many include heart palpitations, dry mouth, or tightness in the throat or chest, which may resemble chronic illness. Although people often fear going to the doctor during mourning, seeing your physician can be quite reassuring. As you learn to deal more satisfactorily with stress in your life, the symptoms that are worrying you are likely to disappear.

If your own health is not a convincing enough argument for giving yourself permission to mourn, let us look to Jewish tradition for a role model. When one of the sons of King David died, David's servants were afraid to tell him about the death. They remembered that, when the child was near death, David's pain

Excerpted from *Mourning and Mitzvah*, 2nd Edition: *A Guided Journal for Walking the Mourner's Path through Grief to Healing* (Jewish Lights) by **Rabbi Anne Brener, LCSW**, professor of ritual and human development at the Academy for Jewish Religion in California.

was so intense that he did not respond to their voices. "How can we tell him the child is dead? He might do something terrible" (2 Samuel 12:18).

Seeing the servants whispering, David asked if the child was dead and was told that this was so.

At that point, David rose, washed, anointed and groomed himself, and prayed. He came into his house and ate the bread that his servants set before him. This surprised them. They pointed out the incongruity of the king fasting and weeping while the child was alive and eating and caring for himself when the child died.

"While the child was still alive," David responded, "I fasted and wept because I thought ... [God] may have pity on me, and the child may live. But now that he is dead, why should I fast? Can I bring him back again? I shall go to him, but he will never come back to me" (2 Samuel 12:22–23).

King David affirmed that, for mourners, life continues, despite the devastating loss. We have the *obligation* of taking care of ourselves. The message is clear in Judaism that we must continue with our lives. As the Book of Deuteronomy says, "I have put before you life and death, blessing and curse. Choose life—if you ... would live" (Deuteronomy 30:19).

Practice: How Do Mourners Behave?

Public images of the mourner enormously influence our understanding of the expectations placed on mourners. King David demonstrated the need to care for oneself after a major tragedy. What other role models do you have? Think about how people you have known or observed have coped with the loss of someone with whom they were close. They may have coped well—or quite poorly. Regardless of how they coped, write about a few people who have contributed to your understanding of how to handle grief. Try especially to remember people you observed in the early years of your life, as you first learned about death. What did you learn from each of these people? Discuss [with a trusted person] how you, as a mourner, are expected to behave and whether those expectations come from society at large, from your own family and friends, or from some other source.

Examining What You Have Learned about Mourning

Remember, we learn from both positive and negative examples. One of my clients spoke resentfully about her recently deceased mother, who frequently burst into tears when remembering her own sister, who had died as a young adult. "The shadow of that aunt hung over everything I did," she angrily told me. "I grew up thinking my life was a tragedy because of an aunt I never knew. I'll never do that to my children."

In a mourning workshop I led, one man described a grandfather who had never ceased grieving for his mother, who had died when he was a child. In another workshop, one participant remembered an aunt who never mentioned the name of the husband who had died in World War II. The way these relatives expressed their losses made a lasting impression.

Your image of mourning may also come through public life or the media. When we hear the word "widow," many of us still see the face of a young Jackie Kennedy, frozen in silent grief. She was credited with great "dignity" in leading our nation through that trauma of her husband's assassination. But I often wonder about the personal cost of her "dignified" and public grief, as well as the danger of a role model who did not shed a public tear.

While still mourning, one of my clients described a very different kind of "widow" when she spoke of being pressured to conform to what she considered to be an oppressive role. "Sometimes," she said, "I feel like Scarlett O'Hara, with her feet secretly tapping to the music of the Virginia reel, hidden below the heavy layers of her black taffeta dress of mourning. I can be walking down the street, feeling just fine, enjoying the chirping of the birds or a beautiful sky, and then I see someone who reminds me that I am supposed to be unhappy."

We are uniquely ourselves. Yet we are also a composite of all of the people who have influenced us. So when we look in the mirror, we also see the images of those who have so profoundly touched our lives that we often mistake their image (and their essence) for our own. During mourning, we have the opportunity to strip away parts of our self-image that are not authentically our own, to bring clarity to our relationships and determine how strongly the deceased has influenced us. As we do this, we begin to reclaim our lives.

Practice: How Did Those Close to You Deal with Intense Feelings?

Think about how significant people in your early life expressed emotion. Do you remember what was said about someone expressing deep feelings? How did you know when someone was angry? How did family members show they were happy or sad? Try to recall specific examples of your family's attitude toward anger, sadness, or joy. How did this affect your ability to express feelings effectively and with satisfaction?

Try to remember how the deceased coped with loss during his or her lifetime. How would he or she expect you to cope with this loss? Describe the deceased's way of expressing grief and other deep feelings, recording, if possible, specific memories that characterized the way you knew what he or she was feeling. You might want to remember an ideal time, when communication and tenderness were at their best. Or you might remember a day when the conflicts that were characteristic of the relationship were clear.

Choosing the Feelings That Are Yours

These attitudes of those to whom you have been close have influenced how you express your own deep emotions. Your father, for example, may have expressed anger explosively, without concern for how this affected others. You may be very much like him, or, after years of being intimidated by him, you may fear your own anger and repress it. It is difficult to predict how we will incorporate the influence of another person. This is often done unconsciously and over many years.

Becoming aware of such influence takes time but may help you find the style of grieving that will be most honest and fruitful for you. Understanding these influences will help you anticipate what mourning might be like for you. You can choose from the positive examples of those who shaped your early emotional life or you can be aware of some of the qualities that you might want to avoid, qualities that you might be prone to during a time of emotional pain, a time when we are all likely to regress emotionally. In the beginning of mourning, memories, even the good ones, are often painful. In your effort to get on with the process of healing, do not forget about the white spaces, even within your own words.[1] Take the time to feel the feelings that these memories generate. If tears come, let them flow. If other feelings come to the surface, do not hold them back. I know that the longing and the despair can be difficult to face. But the feelings are there whether or not you want them to be. Perhaps by facing them something will change.

God's Judgment

Rabbi Kerry M. Olitzky

The Rock, God's work is perfect,
for all God's ways are justice;
a God of faithfulness and without iniquity,
righteous and just is God.

Deuteronomy 32:4

(also part of the *tzidduk hadin*, said at the
cemetery following burial of the deceased)

These are not easy words to say, especially when someone whom we love has died. Yet we recite these words as a reflection of our faith in God even as we suffer the pain of loss. The verse above is part of a longer prayer, probably written during the Talmudic period, that emphasizes the relative worthlessness of humans as compared to God. By reciting this prayer, the mourner declares his or her acceptance of God's harsh decree: the death of a loved one. It is also an acknowledgment that the mourner has realized the limitations of life, something we sometimes forget in our pursuit of the everyday. We are reminded of such things—particularly our own finitude—in the face of death. All else is eclipsed, and often loses meaning, in the presence of death. But in the face of death we are also taught the blessing of our life.

God is known by many names in Jewish tradition. Usually these names are based on our relationship with the Divine. Unlike humans, rocks are eternal. They do not have limited life spans. They were there prior to our death and will be there long after we are gone. But rocks are solid and supportive. Likewise, especially at the time of loss, we depend on God—as a Rock—for support. We lean on God to hold us up when we feel weak and uncertain of ourselves.

Excerpted from *Life's Daily Blessings: Inspiring Reflections on Gratitude for Every Day, Based on Jewish Wisdom* (Jewish Lights) by **Rabbi Kerry M. Olitzky**, executive director of Big Tent Judaism / Jewish Outreach Institute. Rabbi Olitzky's other books include *Grief in Our Seasons: A Mourner's Kaddish Companion* (also Jewish Lights).

What Happens to Us after We Die?

Rabbi Edward Feinstein

If you ask most Americans, you'll find that the question of life after death is the number-one question most people ask of their religion. If you go to the library and check out a book on world religions, you will find that this question is at the very top of the list of important religious questions. It's curious, therefore, that so little attention is given to this question in Jewish life. Visit a church three weeks in a row, and you'll hear two sermons about how we earn life after death. Visit a synagogue for an entire year, and maybe you will hear one mention of heaven, hell, or life after death. Even the Bible doesn't seem to be concerned with the question. In the entire story of Abraham, only four verses tell about his death. Only four verses describe the death of Moses. And there is nothing about their getting into heaven, or anything connected with their life after death.

Life after death is not as important to Judaism as life before death. Life in the "next world" is not as important as life in this world.

Many people use their belief in life after death as a way of escaping concern and responsibility for the condition of this world. After all, they tell themselves, if my life in this world is only temporary and if my life in the "next world" is so much better, why care? Why bother with all the problems here and now? Judaism refuses to let us escape from our responsibility in this world. You and I are God's partners, and we have much to do! The philosopher Abraham Joshua Heschel once remarked, "We Jews believe in another world. We just take our worlds one at a time."

Excerpted from *Tough Questions Jews Ask*, 2nd Edition: *A Young Adult's Guide to Building a Jewish Life* (Jewish Lights) by **Rabbi Edward Feinstein**, senior rabbi at Valley Beth Shalom in Encino, California, and lecturer at American Jewish University. He is also author of *The Chutzpah Imperative: Empowering Today's Jews for a Life That Matters* (also Jewish Lights).

Some religions use their belief in life after death as a way of scaring people: "Believe our way, or else!" Some religious groups offer very detailed descriptions of all sorts of terrible things that await those who refuse to accept their way of doing religion. Judaism believes in a God who created everyone and loves everyone. If there's heaven, you don't have to be Jewish to get there. You have to be a person who has accepted the responsibility of being God's partner. We believe that good people of all religions have a place in the "next world." We've talked about Raul Wallenberg and Sempo Sugihara.[1] Wouldn't you think that God has a special place in heaven for righteous people like them?

Our thinking about afterlife begins with a question about what it means to be human: Am I just a body? If I'm only a body, when my body dies, I die—I'm gone, and nothing lives on. Perhaps there is some part of us which is not body, not physical, so that when we die, this part goes on living.... If I have a soul—or if I am a soul—what's the soul made of? Where does it go when a person dies?

People believe in the soul because of an intuition or a feeling we have that there's more to us than our physical body. We sense that the body is a container, a vessel, for something precious. When my children were born, I had this powerful feeling that there was a whole world of personality packed into that tiny package. When my grandfather died, it was hard to believe that all his wisdom and humor and experience were contained in that very fragile, very delicate container. He was so strong, but his body so weak. He was so big, but his body so small. He was so full of life one moment, and so empty the next.

As with many questions of belief, there isn't just one, but many different Jewish opinions on this question for you to try on:

- There have been Jewish thinkers who believed that we live our lives in this world, and when we die, we die. We live on, in a way, through our families, through the people who remember us, and through all the things we did to make a change in this world.

- Other thinkers proposed that the human being has a soul as well as a body. When we die, our soul returns to God like the wave returning to the ocean.

- Some thinkers have believed that, after death, the soul is judged—rewarded for all the good it did in the world, and punished for all the evil it did. Some have described in very detailed and colorful terms what heaven and hell might be like.

- There are Jewish thinkers who believe that souls are reborn in new bodies and start life all over again. Others believe that souls are stored up with God until a special day comes when all will be reborn—resurrected—to live again, perhaps to live forever in a world without death.

All of these are Jewish beliefs offered by great Jewish thinkers at different times in Jewish history. What they have in common is a belief in a God who loves us, who created us, and who will care for us when we die.

The beliefs in heaven and hell—a life after this one—come from our sadness and anger at all the unfairness in the world. How can we make sense of the contradiction between people's goodness and the terrible things that happen to them in this life? Is it possible that six million Jews were murdered in the Holocaust—their lives stolen from them—and that there is no punishment for those who murdered them? Is it possible that those innocent Jewish victims and the criminals who brought so much pain and destruction are in the same place?

This is a very old question. The Talmud tells a sad story:

A boy was ordered by his father to climb to the top of a tall tree and collect some small birds from a nest. The boy obeyed his father, which fulfilled a commandment of the Torah, "Honor your father and your mother" (Exodus 20:12), and climbed to the treetop. Just before taking the baby birds, the boy shooed away the mother bird. In so doing, he fulfilled another commandment of the Torah, "Do not take the mother together with her young, but let the mother go and take only the young" (Deuteronomy 22:6–7). On the way down the ladder, the boy fell and died.

The Rabbis who witnessed this event were heartbroken. The death of any young person is terrible. But here the boy was in the very process of fulfilling two commandments of the Torah. And more, these are two special commandments—the Torah promises the reward of a long and good life for fulfillment of these two commandments. The Rabbis concluded that the only way to make sense of the world's unfairness—to resolve the contradiction between the

Torah's promise and the events of the world—is to conclude that there is another world, a world of true justice, *olam ha-ba*, a world to come.

Kiddushin 39a

The real question isn't what happens after we die. After all, no one alive knows. We trust that the same God who loves us and gave us life will care for us when we die. The real question is, what do we do until then? How do we live? And if we are concerned about death, we might ask, what can death teach us about living?

The Afterlife and the End of Time

Rabbi Neil Gillman, PhD

Theologies of the afterlife represent our attempt to reinstitute God's power over human life. We affirm that death is not terminal but merely an interim stage in God's ultimate plan for creation. We insist that everything that dies will live again. The English poet John Donne refers to this as the death of death. It is part of the Jewish eschatological dream, the culmination of history in which, among other things, all of humanity will worship the God of Israel, Israel's exile will end, peace will reign, warfare will be abolished, and death shall be no more....

I view death as one more expression of the chaotic element, what the late Milton Steinberg referred to as "the leftover scaffolding of the order of creation." There is so much in this created world that God left undone. There are hurricanes, tornadoes, and earthquakes; there is cancer and other diseases; and there are sudden accidental deaths of children of all ages. Death is one more expression of the inherent absurdity that is left over from the creation of God's world.

Remember that we are dealing with our images of God. There is a way of viewing God as ultimately benevolent, and there is a way of viewing God as ultimately malevolent or perhaps impotent. In *When Bad Things Happen to Good People*, Harold Kushner suggests that the world as a whole is trending ultimately toward the chaotic end of things and that death may simply be part of that broader picture. If this is the case, then our only legitimate human response is to fight the chaos—to fight disease, to fight the earthquake and

---

Excerpted from *Believing and Its Tensions: A Personal Conversation about God, Torah, Suffering and Death in Jewish Thought* (Jewish Lights) by **Rabbi Neil Gillman, PhD**, professor emeritus of Jewish philosophy at The Jewish Theological Seminary. Rabbi Gillman's other books include *The Death of Death: Resurrection and Immortality in Jewish Thought* (also Jewish Lights).

the hurricane, to fight all the forces in the world that are part of what makes life so difficult and painful and that ultimately account for death.

It is striking to me that Judaism incorporated the notion of the afterlife, that the ultimate view of death is that it too will die, and that God's power will assert itself and we will no longer speak of God as vulnerable. This attempt to conquer the chaotic element in creation is the impulse that leads to eschatology. The term "eschatology" refers to study of the last days, the end times. The ultimate purpose of any eschatology is to try to deal with all the anomalies and absurdities that exist in historical time. Eschatology deals with how things will be when historical time has come to an end.

Jewish eschatology happens to be extraordinarily rich. It is as old as scripture and has evolved along with both the history of the Jewish people and the internal evolution of Jewish thinking about the here and now. It deals with three broad topics: what the end of time will be like for the world as a whole, what it will be like for the Jewish people, and what it will be like for the individual human being. For the world as a whole, Jewish eschatology envisions an age of peace, the end of warfare, and the universal recognition of the Jewish people as teaching the Torah to all of humanity. For the Jewish people, it envisions the ingathering of the exiles, the return to Zion, and the rebuilding of the Temple in Jerusalem. For the individual, it envisions the death of death, the end of disease, and the end of everything that stands in the way of human fulfillment.... For this eschatological dream to be in place, death in the here and now cannot be a blessing. It must be one of the obstacles we have to overcome. Judaism has never glorified death. Judaism has always viewed death as a tragedy to be battled in whatever way possible. It will eventually win out in historical time, but ultimately we can dream with John Donne that death too will die.

It should be clear that the realm of eschatology is quite properly a matter of myth, in the classic academic sense of the term. It is not intended to be a factual anticipation of events that will happen in the extended future, but rather an imaginative, subjective construction of an ideal state of affairs that exists properly in the imaginations of the people who conceptualized it. It is classical wishful thinking, designed to give meaning to the course of Israelite history. It is the culminating scenario for the creation story. Creation set the world into motion; eschatology will bring it to an end. It completes the circle.

Eschatology is part of the broad frame in which cosmic history is the portrait. Portraits need a frame. What the frame does is encase the entire scope of the narrative and give it a beginning and an end. If there is no beginning and no end, then there is no middle. If there is no middle, then there is no point of focus, and the picture as a whole loses its intended meaning.

Myths effectively frame our experience. The creation myth at the beginning and the eschatological myth at the end frame the experience of history so that the entire arc of Jewish history now has a focus, an end, and a purpose. Eschatological myths are just as indispensable as creation myths are. Neither is a literal historical event. Both are imaginative constructs designed to provide meaning to the human experience as a whole....

Death remains the ultimate enigma. That is precisely why we need to invoke eschatological myths to deal with it. I can engage with the issue of the existence and nature of God in a more or less coherent way. I can also discuss the theological implications of the revelation of Torah. I can also provide possibly not theological, but at least religious resources for dealing with suffering. Ultimately, however, when I deal with death, I must resort to an eschatological myth. That is probably why it took our ancestors about two thousand years to fashion the eschatological myths that inform our conversation. That is why the conclusion of this chapter leaves me with a sense of theological incompleteness. It is appropriately humbling. It provides a gentle reminder that all of theological speculation is ultimately tension filled. That is probably its greatest contribution.

Does the Soul Survive?

Rabbi Elie Kaplan Spitz

I wish to share with you a journey, my own journey, from denial to acceptance. I begin my story at an annual sermon seminar for rabbis held in
Los Angeles. My overwhelming sense as I prepare to address this audience of
more than eighty rabbis is apprehension. Although I deliver more than one
hundred sermons each year and I have presented to this audience before,
today is different. Today I worry that this assembly will find me gullible, label
me foolish, and question my credibility. Why? My sermon for today is titled
"Why I Now Believe in Survival of the Soul."

For years I squirmed when listening to testimonials of the supernatural. People confided in me, shared remarkable stories surrounding death and dying,
and as their rabbi I listened sympathetically. At the same time, I assumed
that the described events were either coincidences or hallucinations to which
mourners ascribed special meaning as a balm to the pain of loss.

The sermon I was about to deliver emerged from a shift in my own attitude. I had begun to consider these stories of the supernatural more seriously.
This shift occurred a few years earlier, when a series of events drew me to
reconsider whether my reflexive rejection of the supernatural was largely a
means of self-protection from the fear of the unknown. When I began to view
these accounts as real, the many stories fit together like jigsaw puzzle pieces
to form a picture of an otherwise hidden realm of reality. The stories I found
most compelling were those that I heard from people whom I knew and
trusted. In addition, my careful survey of traditional Jewish sources affirmed

Excerpted from *Does the Soul Survive?* 2nd Edition: *A Jewish Journey to Belief in Afterlife,
Past Lives and Living with Purpose* (Jewish Lights) by **Rabbi Elie Kaplan Spitz**, a spiritual leader and scholar specializing in topics of spirituality and Judaism, and rabbi of
Congregation B'nai Israel in Tustin, California. Rabbi Spitz's other books include *Healing from Despair: Choosing Wholeness in a Broken World* (also Jewish Lights).

a faith in survival of the soul that forced me to reconsider my "scientific" assumptions.

As I rise from my seat and walk to the podium I scan the room. Present are some of my favorite teachers and colleagues from Southern California, representing all the major Jewish denominations. We are meeting at Stephen S. Wise Temple, one of Los Angeles's largest and most prestigious congregations, to prepare for our upcoming High Holy Days, Rosh Hashanah and Yom Kippur, the best attended of all the Jewish holidays. My colleagues are seated in the synagogue social hall at long tables behind cups of coffee, danish, and papers covered with notes and doodles.

"Rabbi Yaakov said," I begin while maintaining eye contact with my colleagues, "'This world is like a passageway before the world to come. Prepare yourself so that you might enter into the main banquet room.'[1] These words of the *Ethics of the Fathers*," I emphasize, "are to be taken literally. The passageway is this world and before us is another realm of reality, the world to come."

I describe to my colleagues how over the years I have begun to believe that we possess a soul and that the soul survives this life. As I continue to speak, I gain my stride and relate in an increasingly calm, personal tone stories of graveside mysteries and near-death experiences, describing my sense of discovery. As the emotion in my voice rises, so do my colleagues' heads. They are listening intently as I draw my fifteen-minute talk to a close. I conclude by emphasizing that a belief in survival of the soul only roots us more deeply in living this life each day as a precious gift.

When I finish, hands in the audience shoot up, a rare postsermon occurrence in a synagogue or even at a sermon seminar. Among them is the hand of a senior colleague whom I deeply admire and who is looked to by many of us in the room as a rabbinic role model. I call on him first.

"Isn't such a faith in survival of the soul dangerous?" he asks coolly, with a trace of annoyance in his voice.

The room is still as my colleagues await my reply. I am aware of how rapidly my heart is beating and how adrenaline flows through my system. I take a deep breath and pause.

"Yes," I say. "Faith in the survival of the soul might lead to magical thinking, the belief in an ability to defy reality, and an unrealistic holding on to departed loved ones. But when responsibly approached, faith in the survival of the soul can also be an important source of affirmation and comfort. Like love, such faith is dangerous but no less real."

As I call on other colleagues, their reactions range from firsthand testimonials to uneasiness and skepticism. One rabbi from Orange County, California, who identifies himself as an ardent rationalist, shares the following:

> About ten years ago my wife went into the hospital for routine surgery. Due to a surgical error she developed a life-threatening blood infection, coupled with pneumonia and other complications. The doctors gave her less than a ten percent chance of survival. She had a tube inserted in her throat to aid her with breathing, which prevented her from speaking. When they finally removed her breathing tube, she said, "While I was declining in strength and my pain was increasing, I became aware of all the prayers that people were saying for me. I could actually hear their voices. The prayers formed a cocoonlike structure around me. Each prayer added to the enveloping support. Why is it," she asked, "that our friends the Weisses weren't praying for me?"
>
> What she could not have known was that the Weisses were in Europe around the time that she went in for routine surgery. They did not know she had been gravely ill. I still have no way to explain her uncanny knowledge and the sense that words of prayer had kept her alive.[2]

Another colleague from a large Reform congregation stands up and reports that the previous year he sent a written survey to his congregants asking them to comment on their faith in the supernatural. The responses included many personal anecdotes. He was amazed first by how many people had stories to share and second by his inability to predict based on economic or social background which congregants would offer such accounts.

The feeling in the room is highly charged. I sense that for many participants it is the first time they have publicly shared their stories of the supernatural. An Orthodox rabbi in his sixties approaches the podium and comments that he has never before heard rabbis publicly discuss the supernatural. With a smile, he shares that when he was a psychology major at a leading university many years ago, a prominent teacher announced in the first class, "There are three things you must remember: There is no God, no mind, and no breast-feeding in my class." The rabbi continues, "I am glad that we live in a time of greater openness."

Even after the formal sermon seminar concluded, some of the rabbis continued their discussion. The following day the religion writer for the *Los Angeles Times*, John Dart, called the director of the Board of Rabbis to ask about the seminar. The organizer of the meeting told him that my sermon prompted an animated discussion on survival of the soul. Just as bookstores had begun to place books on the topic of soul and the supernatural on their display tables, Jewish religious leaders were openly discussing a topic that had previously been pushed aside. John Dart interviewed me, and the newspaper story on rabbis debating the supernatural appeared later that week.

Rosh Hashanah approaches, and I prepare to deliver my "Survival of the Soul" sermon to my congregation. The Jewish New Year is a time of contemplation, both of turning inward to renew our spirituality and of turning outward to strengthen our ties to the community. From the pulpit I face my congregants—more than one thousand individuals, mostly conventional professionals raising their families in Orange County, California, a community gradually shifting away from its right-wing tradition. Despite my record of teaching in the community, despite my experience of presenting the same topic at the sermon seminar only one month earlier, and despite the fact that my congregants have come to know and to trust me, I am still filled with anxiety.

As I begin to speak, I seek out the eyes of individuals, searching for a sign of their response. I closely observe the congregation's mood—focused, still. I pace the pulpit, my voice taking on intensity as I strive to convey the central drama: my own awakening to the mysteries of the soul.

When I complete the sermon there are audible sighs in the room. One particularly loud sigh emanates from a key leader in the community. I am unsure if his reaction reflects disbelief or a release from the taut tension of the sermon. Only when the service ends close to two hours later do I receive more specific input. Congregants, including the man with the big sigh, gather around the podium and tell me how appreciative they are of my talk. "Rabbi," one congregant says, "your presentation should be a book. Too many Jews don't know that Judaism believes in the afterlife." Others ask if they can meet me to offer their own stories of soul survival....

In recent years there has been an increased level of interest in survival of the soul. Among the presenters of the supernatural are accomplished physicians and thinkers. Claims of survival of the soul are cross-cultural, span history, and are integrated into most traditional faiths. The increasing interest and faith in survival of the soul may grow into a cultural wave that is as potentially transformative for society as the civil rights movement and feminism. A renewed faith in "the soul's journeys" will call for a reassessment of priorities and enable traditional religions to renew and thereby transform their adherents. Those finding wisdom in Judaism may be encouraged to consider Judaism as the soil on which to nurture spirituality and to thereby elevate their souls.

The increased attention to soul will also change how religious leaders understand and present their own faiths. For most of the past century, rabbis ignored the supernatural or denied it. We were skeptical of anything that could not be seen, controlled, or measured. A soul eludes scientific testing. For years on the pulpit, I also categorized accounts of the paranormal as "twilight zone stories," which I assumed were simply products of wish-fulfilling illusion, superstition, and the movies. I suspected that charlatans who offered easy and false answers to people in pain promoted these phenomena.

In funeral eulogies many rabbis speak of immortality only as the perpetuation of the memory of the departed among the living. Even some of our best rabbis avoid talk about God or reduce God to the best expression of natural processes. There is, however, a growing trend of pausing to reflect on seeming coincidence and the possibility of other realms of human awareness. As a result, there is an increasing faith in the existence of a soul, of an essential part of us that endures.

Broken Open

All Your waves crash over me.

Psalm 88:8

You have cast us off and brought us to confusion.

Psalm 43:10

When a loved one dies, your world changes in ways you could never have foreseen. The shock of loss and grief can leave you numb, breathless, in complete confusion, looking in places you'd never thought to look for answers to questions you never knew you had.

When you are broken open by pain, it is natural to look for comfort in the traditions, relationships, and practices that give life its deepest meaning. Here you will find reflections on confronting chaos, yielding to reality, and taking small, manageable steps to take to help you stay resilient. Even if you are not accustomed to turning to God or Judaism in everyday life, there is no shame in doing so now. As Rabbi Rami Shapiro counsels, God promises to be present when you open up your whole heart to the Divine.

See My Pain

Rebbe Nachman of Breslov

O God,
see my pain.
See the constant tension
and anxiety
with which I must function—
with which I *don't* function.
Touch my life
with Your love,
with Your strength,
with Your wisdom.
I have more than I can bear
alone.

Likutei Moharan 1:54

Excerpted from *The Gentle Weapon: Prayers for Everyday and Not-So-Everyday Moments—Timeless Wisdom from the Teachings of the Hasidic Master, Rebbe Nachman of Breslov* (Jewish Lights), adapted by Moshe Mykoff and S. C. Mizrahi, together with the Breslov Research Institute. **Rebbe Nachman of Breslov** (1772–1810), founder of Breslov Hasidism, is best known for his stories and teachings on mitzvah and relationship with God.

Darkness and Disarray

Rabbi Kerry M. Olitzky

My grandmother used to speak a great deal about the *moloch hamaves,* the angel of death, as she merged Old World stories with an insightful, potently modern understanding of human suffering. And she lived through so much pain herself. This mythic angel reflected real experience and frequently hovered over our family in my childhood and in my adult life, constantly threatening those we loved, even though we tried desperately to keep it at bay. And whenever it struck, our lives were thrown into disarray and the familiar, routine measurement of time lost its meaning. Nights and days often fused together in an undifferentiated blur. Only the mourning process had any relevance or meaning. This kind of chaos occurs even when death is expected, anticipated, even welcomed, after a long illness or a hospital stay.

Jewish tradition tells us to stop everything that we are doing, acknowledge God, rend our garments, and immediately start the mourning process so we can find our mooring and stability when we need it most. As soon as a loved one dies, the details of our daily lives become essentially irrelevant and lose their importance. It is the process of mourning, the result of the evolution of Jewish ritual over time, that helps us reorganize our lives and establish a new rhythm for daily living.

The Torah tells us that the world was *tohu vavohu* ("dark and in disarray") prior to God's work of creation. Then "God's spirit hovered over the earth" and brought order out of the chaos. Set into motion, the world followed a certain order or set pattern (what the rabbis call *olam kenegdo*), something that we come to expect, something on which we depend. But just as this

Excerpted from *Grief in Our Seasons: A Mourner's Kaddish Companion* (Jewish Lights) by **Rabbi Kerry M. Olitzky**, executive director of Big Tent Judaism / Jewish Outreach Institute. Rabbi Olitzky's other books include *Life's Daily Blessings: Inspiring Reflections on Gratitude for Every Day, Based on Jewish Wisdom* (also Jewish Lights).

order is never like it was at Creation, our lives really never again return to the way they once were. This sense of disarray and disorder lies under the surface of even what appears to be orderly. And we are forced to find our way through it—guided by God and by Jewish tradition.

Praying in Crisis

Rabbi Mike Comins

I remember after the Asian Tsunami hearing someone say, "How can these people believe in God anymore? How can they even pray? They've lost everything, everyone, not even a photograph of their loved ones exists, everything is gone, and yet they pray!" And another responded, "They've lost everything, and now you want to take God away from them, too?" I was really struck by this answer. I have been through many troubling and trying times, and have accompanied people when their paths became burdensome and nearly unbearable, and I have noticed a difference between people who try to muster some relationship with God in crises and those who have always been in relationship with God. Those who have always been in relationship can lean more easily on God, and can speak more freely, expressing their hope as well as their anger. I have seen prayer help people overcome loss, deal with grief, change their direction, and recover, but usually it is in people who have become practiced in prayer through their own rituals and devotion to it. It is not usual that someone prays for the first time and their life is altered, although sometimes it can happen, rare as revelation.

Rabbi Zoë Klein

...

It would be nice if God would come down and explain to us why life is unfair and why innocent people suffer and why the world is filled with both great beauty and great pain, but so far God hasn't

---

Excerpted from *Making Prayer Real: Leading Jewish Spiritual Voices on Why Prayer Is Difficult and What to Do about It* (Jewish Lights) by **Rabbi Mike Comins**, founder of TorahTrek Spiritual Wilderness Adventures and author of *A Wild Faith: Jewish Ways into Wilderness, Wilderness Ways into Judaism* (Jewish Lights).

explained it. There are times when prayer does not solve the problem. There are times when I can't feel God. And I don't know what to pray and I don't sense God's presence. I just don't. I understand why people hang up the phone until they're ready to call again. That's part of my story.

Rabbi Naomi Levy

I would never judge one who told me that they couldn't pray, especially when facing significant pain or loss. And yet, I would recommend it. If we can gather the strength, spiritual practice from the midst of crisis is a unique opportunity to move down the spiritual path and mature as a human being.

I remember teaching a class on Job, and as people spoke, it became clear. Nobody took the class out of academic interest. Everyone was dealing with loss. Surprisingly, most people reported that their faith was strengthened by the experience. Finally, my friend Debbie Mell asked, "Does anyone get to God without a crisis, without suffering?"

I'm sure there are people who do, but it seems to me that more people discover God, rather than lose God, when they suffer. As a liberal Jew, I am not surrounded by people who would blame God for a disease, let alone a divorce. So perhaps it is not surprising. But secular critics claim that people turn to God in times of crisis as a crutch. Are these people turning to God out of desperation?

Not from what I can tell, and not from my own experience. Neither the liberals nor the traditionalists I know think that God will solve their problems for them by waving a wand. Rather, when crisis hits, we are stripped of so much of who we are. The death of loved ones, illness, divorce, the loss of a job: suddenly we can no longer live the way we were just a short time before. The future is unknown. Against our will, the psychological safety net, and sometimes our physical security as well, have been torn from us. Our expectations about how the world works are no longer valid. Most painful of all, our self-image has shattered. We are vulnerable, exposed, and searching for a new path.

Why don't people change? It is often too difficult to risk letting go of the patterns and defense mechanisms, psychological and physical, that keep us safe. Better to stick with some bad habits than suffer uncertainty. But in times of crisis, the familiar patterns are taken from us whether we like it or not. If we can be with the pain without losing ourselves—if we can get some perspective—opportunity knocks. We are given the possibility of changing for the better. For when we are searching, we are more receptive to new ways of living in the world. And when we are vulnerable and exposed, we might find ourselves willing to hear voices we previously blocked out. We might receive the support of sources we refused to consider in the past. We might discover God.

Struggling with Reality

Rabbi Karyn D. Kedar

How many times will we recount the renaming of our patriarch Jacob who struggled with a stranger, an angel of God, in the middle of the night? Like children who look at a family album, we seem to say, "Tell me the story again. How did we become the people of Israel, the great strugglers?" ...

And so we tell the story of how Jacob wrestled with a stranger, some say an Angel of God, and how he was wounded from the fight. And we learn that sometimes when we wrestle with God, when we shake our fists at the heavens yelling "What was that about?" sometimes we are wounded. In the name of God people are killed, lives destroyed. People are in pain and sometimes lives are destroyed.

It is hard to suffer. It is even harder to love those who suffer. It is maddening to watch those who are insane with misled religious zeal destroy without sense or reason. Life challenges our sense of fairness, justice, and basic right. It simply is not right that a young mother die of breast cancer. It is not right that her teenage children are thrown into a world where spiritual and emotional survival are an overwhelming challenge. It is not right that her husband should wander through life not finding love and peace for years after her death.

God-listening is a tricky business fraught with dangers. To be a person of faith takes courage and a limber sense of reason. Belief in God and the fundamental goodness of life often contrasts sharply with the events of our lives. Jacob teaches us that if we wrestle with God, we are in good company, for we are the children of Israel.

Excerpted from *Our Dance with God: Finding Prayer, Perspective and Meaning in the Stories of Our Lives* (Jewish Lights) by **Rabbi Karyn D. Kedar**, spiritual counselor, inspirational speaker, and senior rabbi at Congregation B'nai Jehoshua Beth Elohim in Chicago. Rabbi Kedar's other books include *The Bridge to Forgiveness: Stories and Prayers for Finding God and Restoring Wholeness* (also Jewish Lights).

Today the sunlight invited me to walk a slow uncharted mile where the only sound I heard was the soft crackle of my step against the autumn leaves. My mind wandered along with my path until I had a thought that soon became louder than any other sound and repeated itself over and over. I thought: "I don't believe that God exists in theoretical discourse or philosophical proofs. Rather, God is experienced, if allowed, in the soft spots of the human heart. Softness that sometimes hurts like a bruise or an open wound and sometimes is so soft that you feel as if you are warmed by fine cashmere."

Soft spots. The soul. The spirit of a human life. The Divine within. All are words and phrases describing a sense we have that there must be more than the physical world, more than the body and even the mind. These words describe the struggle we have to discover meaning and purpose, the struggle we have to connect with the divine intention for our lives. I believe that God can be experienced in that internal spot, which is ever so soft and vulnerable....

Why is it that the tenacity of the human spirit, the overwhelming beauty of nature, the miracle of birth, the simple joy of first snow falling silently at midnight are not enough to sustain a belief in God? Tragedy and sadness seem to have more force and power and often banish faith and belief for generations. This is why I am drawn to loss and sadness—to understand the power they have to break or strengthen faith, to bear witness to those who have experienced the unthinkable and yet whose faith has survived.

I feel compelled to tell their stories. For you ask, so very often with tears in your eyes and fear in your hearts, where was God when my mother suffered with cancer? Where is God in the silent boredom of my life? Where was God during the Holocaust? It's not for me to answer. I listen to you, the survivors. Because ultimately you are right: If your faith in God cannot sustain you in your pain, who needs it?

... Living a life that includes the demands and commands of the spiritual world is a challenge. It is a struggle to reconcile reality with the tender yearning and dreams of the heart. This world that we have created, this life that we have been granted, confronts us with dramatic struggles on a regular basis. Perhaps that's really the reason we have stopped listening: it is too much of a struggle. And yet, with the spiritual world muted, we become strangers to meaning and purpose. *Shema Yisrael*: Hear, you strugglers with God.

Resiliency

Rabbi Shira Stern, DMin, BCC

Some people are born resilient; they always land on their feet despite any and all obstacles in their path. They manage their bad news, disappointments, and disasters with remarkable aplomb. But what about the rest of us, who are scared and confused and helpless when plans go awry? Is there a way for us to experience trauma or stress or difficulties and respond to them in a healing fashion? Can we learn something from the lives of others that will inform *our* behavior, so that we survive our bad breaks more readily? And is there a way to do more than survive—actually to thrive—in life?

It is difficult to define resilience, because it is much more than simply the "power or ability to return to the original form, position, etc., after being bent, compressed, or stretched; [in other words, the definition of] elasticity."[1] Human beings cannot be unaffected by trauma; we are not as malleable as stress balls, and, contrary to the dictionary definition, we also never revert to our "original form." We bear the scars, both internal and external, of trauma and misfortune. And, sadly, we do not always have "the ability to recover readily from illness, depression, adversity, or the like."[2] We are certainly not always characterized by "buoyancy."[3] We carry with us the memories of the day or moment or, sometimes, the prolonged agony of a loved one hanging on to life.

I found great resonance in Carole Radziwill's memoir entitled *What Remains: A Memoir of Fate, Friendship, and Love*. Having lost three loved ones within a three-week period—her husband at thirty-six, his first cousin, and her best friend—she had come to realize that the key to resiliency was reestablishing balance after your world implodes.[4]....

Excerpted from *Judaism and Health: A Handbook of Practical, Professional and Scholarly Resources* (Jewish Lights), edited by Jeff Levin, PhD, MPH, and Michele F. Prince, LCSW, MAJCS. **Rabbi Shira Stern, DMin, BCC**, is founding director of the Center for Pastoral Care and Counseling in Marlboro, New Jersey.

In my own search for resiliency, I have learned these lessons from unexpected sources. In reading through how the Army addresses the issue of spiritual resiliency, I found this image of "breathing cadences," which resonated deeply for me:

> When we run during physical training, we often sing familiar cadences to keep pace. Those cadences or "Jodie calls" not only keep us in step, but they also help facilitate our breathing as we run. The Army's current operational tempo has called us all to join in a long distance run of heart and soul that requires discipline, perseverance, and deep breathing to finish successfully. Wayne Cordeiro does a great job in his book *Leading on Empty* of describing the need for a spiritual leader to maintain a "life cadence" that includes daily, weekly and monthly spiritual practices that maintain the pace and depth of their spiritual lives. Are you "in step with the spirit" as you run this long race of leadership? Do you count off a "life cadence" that helps you maintain the pace of leadership in this midst of the high velocity challenge in which God's called you to serve? Your answers to those questions are gauges to the reality of your resilience. Each of us possesses the potential to establish those "cadences" so that we continue to receive the inspiration to bounce back and push further ahead in our spiritual missions.[5]

Each morning, the daily liturgy provides us with the words to articulate our gratitude that our soul, our breath, has been returned to us to enable us to survive.

Sometimes I find myself weak and scared, and lonely, and depressed. At other times, even after a long day during which I felt I only put out fires and did not accomplish what I intended to do, I feel good. At the very least, I have addressed the issues that are important to me, or, as Viktor Frankl said, "Man is *not* fully conditioned and determined but rather determines himself whether he gives into conditions or stands up to them."[6]

It is not easy to stand up to difficult conditions or tragedy or trauma. And most of us have felt like we are hanging on to this life by a thread, whether it is for a moment or some protracted time. Resilience is not the constant bright light that shines our way ahead; it is getting up each day to rekindle the tiny flame. Rabbi Steven Kushner points out that *the* original eternal light was not eternal at all; it required the Israelites to renew the oil and the wick *each and every day*. The same thing is required of our own light: day after day, whether we anticipate great joy or we dread what is about to happen, we wake up and reignite the flame. Sometimes that is about all the energy that we can muster. Sometimes it is the starting point for a great move forward.

Being Present to God

Translated and Annotated by Rabbi Rami Shapiro

The One Who Is says:
I know the plans I have set for you:
plans for your welfare, not your destruction.
My desire is for a future filled with hope.
When you call Me,
when you follow Me,
when you pray to Me,
I will listen.
When you seek Me you will find Me,
providing that you seek Me with a whole heart.

Jeremiah 33:3

What is God's listening? It is God fully present to you in, as, and at this very moment. God is always present. The question is: Are you? A whole heart is a heart that holds nothing back. Do not imagine you must be a certain way with God; that you must feel faithful and trusting; that you must overcome doubt, anger, and fear. Seek God through your imperfections and confusion. Without changing anything, turn your whole self to God, and let God change everything.

Excerpted from *The Hebrew Prophets: Selections Annotated and Explained* (SkyLight Paths) by **Rabbi Rami Shapiro**, a renowned teacher of spirituality across faith traditions and an award-winning storyteller, poet, and essayist. Rabbi Shapiro's other books include *Amazing Chesed: Living a Grace-Filled Judaism* (Jewish Lights).

Yearning for God

Rabbi Nancy Flam

I grew up in a household that didn't talk about God. When I entered adolescence, my yearnings for depth, connection, and truth began to intensify. Only later did I come to understand that these yearnings were part of a search for God's presence in my life and that I was not alone in my search. When I began to study religion in college, I found others who were eager to talk about their ideas and experiences of God's reality. Somewhere in my sophomore year, I dared to consider that my growing sense of wonder, mystery, beauty, and compassion had something to do with God. I began to believe that, in fact, I had a very strong connection to God. Exploring, cultivating, and deepening this relationship with God has been at the center of my life ever since.

I can't say that the path is easy. There are times of great disconnection, times when I feel spiritually asleep, times when I question my own experience of God's reality. And yet, despite the challenges, I find that my central desire is to know God's presence: to cultivate an open, responsive heart; to be alert to the vitality within and around me; to experience myself as part of an interconnected whole; and to recognize the beauty and mystery of creation.

We experience yearning for God in many ways. Sometimes our yearning begins with an underlying sense of emptiness or shallowness. We may feel that we are lost or that something is missing. There sometimes grows in us a desire for a greater fullness and vitality in our lives. We seek to fill an emptiness; many of us try to fill ourselves with excessive food, alcohol, drugs, or distraction of one kind or another (such as TV, movies, computers, excessive sex). Often, we are unaware that our deeper desire is for a relationship with

Excerpted from *Yearning for God*, a LifeLight™ pastoral care pamphlet (Jewish Lights) by **Rabbi Nancy Flam**, founding director of the Institute for Jewish Spirituality and cofounder of the Jewish Healing Center.

God: a relationship in which we might discover profound beauty, worth, and meaning.

For many of us, our yearning for God is activated at a particular crossroads in our lives: when our physical or mental health is challenged, after the loss of a loved one, or in the midst of a life change such as marriage, divorce, or the birth of children. We yearn for God as a source of comfort, hope, or perspective. We seek the assurance that our lives make sense and that, on some ultimate level, everything will be all right....

Our yearning for God does not get sated once and for all. We all know periods when our relationship with God is best characterized by a flat absence. At such times, our hearts resonate with the words of the psalmist who wrote, "I am weary with calling, my throat is dry; my eyes fail while I wait for God" (Psalm 69:4). At these times, God is simply eclipsed from us. At other times, often by surprise, we feel God's presence gracing our lives with meaning, clarity, vitality, and gentleness. We open to the beauty of the world; our hearts soften and bring us into blessed relationship with all that is within and around us. But inevitably, such moments fade. We find ourselves again yearning to sense God's nearness. Perhaps it is out of a recognition of the ebb and flow of our relationship with God that the psalmist wrote, "One thing I ask of God; only that do I seek: to live in the house of God all the days of my life, to gaze upon the beauty of God and to meditate in God's sanctuary" (Psalm 27:4).

Responding to Suffering

Rabbi Dayle A. Friedman, MSW, MA, BCC

I n responding to suffering, the first, immense step is to accept reality. A great Hasidic sage, the Gerer Rebbe, teaches in his commentary *Sefat Emet* (Language of Truth) that even in moments of darkness we can connect to the vital divine power hidden within us by "submitting ourselves before truth" (1:246). We can stiffen and resist the truth of our lives, or we can soften to it. This is not easy or even intuitive—I would certainly prefer to run away from darkness. I guess I am attached to the illusion of control, and I balk at the idea of submitting myself to anything.

Nonetheless, my work with aging people has dramatically demonstrated to me that we are *not* in control; much of what life brings us is not up to us. As we grow older, we face so many unwelcome realities: we lose our dearest companions; we may find new limits on our energy; we will most likely encounter physical frailty; friends or family members may disappoint us; roles that we cherished may evaporate; we may need assistance for tasks we once managed independently. But denial and resistance may be our reflexive response. "I can still do that." "I don't need help." When we resist painful reality, we add to our suffering (and often to that of the people around us). How many families have struggled when an elder who, like my dad, clearly was no longer capable but insisted on continuing to drive? How many baby boomers have avoided thinking about growing older and thus failed to save money for retirement? As the Buddhist teacher Pema Chödrön writes in her book *The Places That Scare You: A Guide to Fearlessness in Difficult Times*, "Never underestimate our inclination to bolt when we hurt."[1]

Excerpted from *Jewish Wisdom for Growing Older: Finding Your Grit and Grace Beyond Midlife* (Jewish Lights) by **Rabbi Dayle A. Friedman, MSW, MA, BCC**, who offers training, consulting, and spiritual guidance through Growing Older, her Philadelphia-based national practice. Rabbi Friedman is also editor of *Jewish Pastoral Care: A Practical Handbook from Traditional and Contemporary Sources* (also Jewish Lights).

This business of yielding to unwelcome reality is so hard. It is natural, reflexive, to deny, to stiffen. When you pull a muscle in your back, your body responds with alarm. Your body attempts to protect the hurt, raw place by hardening around it. You want to make sure that nothing can get to that vulnerable place and injure it further. But a strange thing happens. Instead of feeling better, now you are not only sore but also stiff. You find you have trouble bending, turning, and eventually moving at all. You want to take to your bed; you pray that this will all just pass. Surprisingly, you should do anything *but* this. Stretch, move gently, your doctor tells you, and you will heal. This is yielding....

To soften to reality, we need to allow ourselves to feel hurt and grief. In this yielding to *what is*, we are liberated from the burden of resisting. We might just find ourselves able to perceive and pursue new possibilities.

Practice: Reflecting on Reality

We can gently invite ourselves to face that which we are avoiding, thus opening ourselves to choices and goodness rather than putting down the burden of resistance and hardening ourselves. This practice of reflection can be a starting place.

Do this when you have at least twenty minutes.

Sit comfortably. Breathe naturally and allow your body to relax as much as possible. Take some time to reflect on at least one of the following realms of your life:

- Intimate relationships: partner, parents, children, siblings
- Work
- Home
- Physical health
- Religious/spiritual life

Ask yourself whether there is something you are avoiding acknowledging or are resisting. If you become aware of something, notice the resistance. What does it feel like in your body? Is there an image or a metaphor that describes it? Allow the resistance to "talk to you": What would be the worst thing that might happen if you faced the truth? What would be the best? Can you invite yourself to open a bit?

See whether there is a hope that you have about this reality. If you wish, you can express that hope as a prayer, on the order of the following:

> Source of life [or whatever name for the Divine suits you] who has sustained my ancestors and me, help me to face _____. Give me strength and courage, and guide me on this path whose direction I cannot yet see. Open me to the reality before me; help me to be whole.

A Blessing

May you face suffering with grit and grace. May you learn to see the truth of your experience. May you find the strength to understand where you are in times of darkness. And may you wrest sweetness from your pain.

Crying Out

I will give full vent to my complaint;
I will speak in the bitterness of my soul.

Job 10:1

Grief contains so many other emotions along with sorrow: Anger that no one stopped this loss from happening. Anguish in your aloneness. Despair of the world ever making sense again. Frustration that no one seems to understand. Disbelief that the universe has betrayed your trust. Rage at the platitudes people try to offer you for comfort.

Be assured that you are very much not alone. As you read these prayers and laments, join your voice to those who have suffered such anguish before. May you find here healing ways to express everything that's in your heart.

Thou Shalt Not Take the Name

Rabbi Nancy Fuchs-Kreimer, PhD

Despite popular impression, the Book of Job does not focus on the question: Why do the righteous suffer? The very beginning of the book disposes of that issue. Job suffers because the Accuser made a bet with God. The Book of Job is about a different query: How shall we talk about God in the midst of a suffering world? How shall we talk *to* God?...

"God damn!" I blurted out. I was a ten-year-old reaching for words to express my indignation at having stubbed my toe. It was just a phrase I had heard, something to say when angry. My mother, rewinding a rusty tape recorder in her brain, pushed PLAY: "Thou shalt not take the name of thy Lord in vain." I was dumbfounded. Everyday I was admonished to be kind, to share with my brother and sister, to tell the truth. These were presented as the right things to do. The "Lord" was never brought into the discussion. Come to think of it, God was not mentioned at all, for any reason. My mother seemed less concerned about this rule than about kindness and truth-telling. No wonder she resorted to the archaic language of the Bible. This was a rule that made no sense except in context. (If there is no God, what does it matter how we use "His" name?)

Actually, this had very little to do with God. It was about being proper and appropriate, not rude and out of line. But mostly it was about getting angry. What was bad about cursing, I concluded, was that it shows you are angry, which you should not be. When you are angry, keep it to yourself. Better still,

---

Excerpted from *Broken Tablets: Restoring the Ten Commandments and Ourselves* (Jewish Lights), edited by Rachel S. Mikva. **Rabbi Nancy Fuchs-Kreimer, PhD**, is director of the department of multifaith studies and initiatives and associate professor of religious studies at Reconstructionist Rabbinical College. Rabbi Fuchs-Kreimer is also coauthor of *Judaism for Two: A Spiritual Guide for Strengthening and Celebrating Your Loving Relationship* (also Jewish Lights).

don't become angry at all. But in the meantime, I was intrigued. Who is this "Lord" and why did it matter so much to people how "His" name was used?

> Now Job had three friends—Eliphaz the Temanite, Bildad the Shuhite, and Zopher the Namathite. When these friends heard of all the calamities that had come upon him, each of them left his own country to mourn with Job and to comfort him.

I was thirteen, blessedly untouched by death, attending my first funeral. Great Uncle Al left his shocked and terrified widow, and two children not much older than I. This was something new to me. But even newer was the theology of the freelance rabbi hired by the funeral home for the occasion. He provided a clumsy compendium of "it's all for the best," promises of the afterlife, and "it could have been worse." (From the rabbi's point of view, that last statement was strictly true; it could have happened to him.)

I was devastated. Not by the death, but by the rabbi. Such *vain* comfort. How dare this rabbi bring God into all this sadness and in such a patently unbelievable fashion? I had come to the conclusion that God is the sum of all that is good and wondrous in the world; now God's name was being misused for what I believed to be false consolation. This, I concluded, is what it means to take God's name in vain. Oblivious to the fact that at the time there were no rabbinical schools that accepted women, I decided then and there to become a rabbi....

> God damn the day I was born and the night that forced me from the womb.

This sentence, uttered by Job as his opening volley, might well qualify as the most blasphemous statement in the Bible: cursing God by cursing God's greatest gift—life. One thing is clear. This is a statement of anger, and a statement of acknowledgment: God is about evil. So, we acknowledge—first in anger and then, if we are graced to sit with it long enough, perhaps in another key.

The Talmud says that a person is known by his pocket, his cup, and his rage. Perhaps if we can be with our rage, we can see it form itself anew as a serenity of sorts and we will emerge more compassionate and more generous.

Perhaps we will even be able to laugh again. Recall the midrash written by shocked and sorrowing Jews after their defeat by the Romans. What were they to do with the verse, "Who is like You among the gods (*elim*)?" One rabbi suggested slightly reworking it to read, "Who is like You among the mute (*ilemim*)?" That, at least, was frank. Resigned, but still feisty. A person is known by his humor as well as by his anger.

A friend of mine visited her mother, who is a Holocaust survivor and an Orthodox Jew. Sitting in the park together, they heard one of her mother's friends talking. "What a beautiful wedding I went to last night. The *chassen* (groom) was a mensch, a gentle young man, so sweet and for once he wasn't sleeping." My friend could not understand why the *chassen* would be sleeping, but the woman clarified her words. She was not referring to the groom but to God: "*Er shluft a sach* (He sleeps a lot)." This observant Jewish woman knew what God was supposed to do. She also knew what she knew about life. She refused to gloss over her own truth, so she told a story that makes sense to her of the way things seem to go. There is a great, mighty, and awesome God ruling the universe but He sleeps a lot. The psalmist asked, "Why do You sleep?" (Psalm 44:24). She was not bothering to ask that question anymore, but she was prepared to bless the moments when, against all odds, joy seemed to be breaking through.

> The Lord said to Eliphaz the Temanite, "I am very angry at you and your two friends, because you have not spoken the truth about Me as my servant Job has.... My servant Job will pray for you and for his sake I will overlook your sin."

In the end, God seems to appreciate his apologists very little. God does, however, appear to value honesty.... We must speak from the depths of our experience, of our feelings, of our hearts and acknowledge it all: the God who, like a doting grandparent, treasures our every gesture and the one who, as Shakespeare noticed, like a wanton boy with flies, kills us for sport.

Say it all out loud. Care about getting it right. Hold on to all your joy— and to all your hurt. Ignore mealy-mouthed defenses of God that leave you taking the blame. Avoid people who have anything too quick and pious to say about God. Pray you can reach a place where the good and the evil can be heard in stereo and the music will sound sweet.

Where Is God When We Feel Alone?

Rabbi Daniel F. Polish, PhD

There are times in every life when God seems hidden, when the warmth and nurture we desire and need is replaced by cold darkness. At these times our prayers cannot be of thanksgiving, praise, or even petition. All that we can do is cry out, like a person separated from his or her traveling companions in a strange and vaguely threatening environment, "Where are you?"

When we are in its grip, this sense of abandonment can feel like something unique to ourselves. It is not. And it is not something that any of us should feel ashamed of. Sometimes when we experience this feeling we ask ourselves if we are losing our faith in God or ceasing to be a religious person. Actually the opposite is true. The sense of pain or anguish at what feels like the absence of God is its own profound kind of religiousness. It is a special way of relating to God, one that bears witness to the intensity and importance of that relationship in our own lives—just as only those who love each other can feel deeply the pangs of separation. Anguish at God's separation from us is not a rejection of God, but a deeply emotional testimony to the role that God plays in our lives....

The Psalms make repeated use of the powerful image of God's face being hidden from us. Admittedly, today we tend to be uncomfortable with anthropomorphic images that speak of God in terms of human attributes. Yet this image does strike a chord in us. It feels to us that God is not merely away, but is holding back from us, hiding. Like the face of the sun hidden by clouds, or during an eclipse, God's face feels hidden from us in our time of need.

Excerpted from *Bringing the Psalms to Life: How to Understand and Use the Book of Psalms* (Jewish Lights) by **Rabbi Daniel F. Polish, PhD**, spiritual leader of Congregation Shir Chadash. Rabbi Polish's other books include *Keeping Faith with the Psalms: Deepen Your Relationship with God Using the Book of Psalms* (also Jewish Lights).

Paradoxically, these verses from Psalms bring a particular kind of comfort to us because they assure us that we are not alone in feeling cut off from God when we need God's presence. Others experience this same eclipse, the Psalms remind us; people have anguished over it for thousands of years....

Psalm 88 gives us a good insight into the powerful dialectic of Psalms. Clearly it is the cry of one who feels abandoned.

2 O Lord, God of my salvation,
   What time I cry in the night before Thee,
3 Let my prayer come before Thee,
   Incline Thine ear unto my cry.
4 For my soul is sated with troubles,
   And my life draweth nigh unto the grave.
5 I am counted with them that go down into the pit;
   I am become as a man that hath no help;
6 Set apart among the dead,
   Like the slain that lie in the grave,
   Whom Thou rememberest no more;
   And they are cut off from Thy hand.
7 Thou hast laid me in the nethermost pit,
   In dark places, in the deeps.
8 Thy wrath lieth hard upon me,
   And all Thy waves Thou pressest down.
9 Thou hast put mine acquaintance far from me;
   Thou hast made me an abomination unto them;
   I am shut up, and I cannot come forth.
10 Mine eye languisheth by reason of affliction;
   I have called upon Thee, O Lord, every day,
   I have spread forth my hands unto Thee.
11 Wilt Thou work wonders for the dead?
   Or shall the shades arise and give Thee thanks?
12 Shall Thy mercy be declared in the grave?
   Or Thy faithfulness in destruction?
13 Shall Thy wonders be known in the dark?
   And Thy righteousness in the land of forgetfulness?
14 But as for me, unto Thee, O Lord, do I cry,
   And in the morning doth my prayer come to meet Thee.

¹⁵Lord, why castest Thou off my soul?
  Why hidest Thou Thy face from me?
¹⁶I am afflicted and at the point of death from my youth up;
  I have borne Thy terrors, I am distracted.
¹⁷Thy fierce wrath is gone over me;
  Thy terrors have cut me off.
¹⁸They came round about me like water all the day;
  They compassed me about together.
¹⁹Friend and companion hast Thou put far from me,
  And mine acquaintance into darkness.[1]

This psalm is almost unbearably painful to read. You can feel the piercing anguish of one who feels abandoned. As we read it, we feel our way into the author's emotions. We cry out to God, pour out our troubles. And yet, what makes those troubles harder to bear is the sense that God is somehow at the root of our problems. Certainly our fellow human beings have not helped us (verses 9, 19), but could it be that God is somehow responsible for that distance? Even more darkly, the psalm suggests that God is responsible for all the misfortunes that have befallen us (verses 7–8). Indeed, the psalmist fears that it is possible that God is angry at us (verses 8, 17)....

Once we recognize the undertone to these verses we can also note that they constitute the beginning of movement from out of the pit of our despair. Here the reversal of fortune begins, for the significant thing about these feelings of alienation is not that we have them, but that we move beyond them. To move toward healing we must first acknowledge that we feel ourselves cut off, abandoned.... The next step is for us to move from a sense of God's distance to the sense that we can call on God for help. That is what the series of verses above do. They begin, timidly enough, to enlist God as a helper. God becomes involved in our situation and enrolled in our cause. After all, *what good am I to You, if I have entered the domain of death?*... The sense of utter abandonment at the beginning of the psalm gives way to hope of divine aid.

The psalmist marks out the road that each of us can travel to move beyond our sense of abandonment and alienation to a renewed sense of God's presence and potential for partnership. That impassioned cry for God's help can become our own as we read this psalm and others like it. It can become our most sincere prayer in our darkest times.

Immobilized by Anger and Fear

Rabbi James L. Mirel and Karen Bonnell Werth

Emotional pain may be the loneliest illness since there is often no outward manifestation of the painful inner world, no outward signaling system (like broken bones, wounds, fevers) to alert others to our needs. When experiencing painful emotions, it is important that we have some way to make sense out of our feelings and find constructive ways to resolve the pain. While this is not always easy, our spiritual work can strengthen our emotional resilience and expand our coping mechanisms.

Anger is like a fire that burns in our bellies when we feel disappointed, hurt, or betrayed. A natural and powerful response to injustice, anger can be constructive and energizing, preparing us for action. Or it can be destructive and consume our thinking, leading to impulsive actions that might be hurtful or violent. Learning to respect the power of anger and channel it constructively is an important part of the spiritual path. We can transform anger into creative problem solving and action, but doing so requires examining our feelings and praying for wisdom and insight. It's important to assess the effects of our words and actions and determine if we are responding out of vindictiveness or out of justice.

Harboring our anger and turning it inward on itself may be toxic to the body and spirit. Being angry dramatically changes our perceptions of life, making us feel uneasy and distrustful. Like any "power," the use of anger must not be taken lightly. It requires mindfulness and deep concern for its effect on ourselves, on others, and on the world.

Excerpted from *Stepping Stones to Jewish Spiritual Living: Walking the Path Morning, Noon, and Night* (Jewish Lights) by **Rabbi James L. Mirel**, rabbi emeritus of Temple B'nai Torah in Bellevue, Washington, and **Karen Bonnell Werth**, a health-care professional and developer of the yearlong facilitator training program for the Compassionate Listening Project.

One of the consequences of monotheism is that everything is ultimately attributed to God. While Rabbinic and Christian theology envisioned Satan as a possible source of some of the "evil" in the world, the Hebrew Bible clearly asserts that God is the source of everything. But while anger is a universal human reality, another universal reality is the destructive power of nature. To the biblical mind, the power of nature could only be attributed to a monumental divine anger. But if we read the Bible solely as theology, we make a grave mistake. The Torah is a compendium of an entire worldview, and God is its central reality, but it also consists of human perception. In the biblical mind, everything has a justification. While God is the force behind all reality, it is people who, through their free will, can become angry, violent, and destructive....

Another difficult, often immobilizing emotion is fear. It can keep us from creating, exploring, expressing, and loving fully. In order to be open to our potential as co-creators, to step directly into our purpose in life, we must face our fears: fears about what others think, about money, about acceptance/rejection, about ability, about making a mistake, about taking a risk, about *who we are*. We are made in the divine image; we are children of God; we are co-creators; we are capable of living fully and mindfully in God's Light. Letting go of fear (to whatever degree we can) and trusting ourselves, trusting God, and moving forward is our spiritual work. As Psalm 23:4 states, "I fear not, for You are with me; Your guidance and blessings comfort me."

Fear of God as expressed in the Bible refers to awe and reverence for the power of God, which is the power of the Life Force. This "fear" was seen as the motivation for obedience to God. Today we also may be motivated to obey Torah—the spiritual laws that guide life—out of similar awe and reverence for the Power of Creation. In prayer, we find that the word "fear" is related to separation from God since our deep love of God and our wish for closeness evoke a fear that we might be estranged from the Divine Source of Life.

Fear is a deeply rooted human emotion. Coupled with anxiety, it can cripple our well-being. Accepting ourselves, learning to love and honor ourselves, trusting our inner knowing, and finding security in our place in creation will assist with decreasing fear and opening to Life—to God.

Personal Reflection: The Power of Emotions

They say my grandmother "died of a broken heart" after the death of her son, my uncle, in a fire during World War II. I've come to understand that the shock, anger, and sadness of the news was followed by a fatal heart attack—the literal destruction of her heart. Only God knows whether the news of my uncle's death had any bearing on her heart attack. Sometimes I hear people say, "I was scared to death" or "I was so angry I couldn't see straight." All these expressions remind me what a powerful role emotion plays in our physical, emotional, and spiritual well-being. When feelings are overwhelming, we do whatever we can to make sense out of our experience, to find cause and effect. We may try to justify how we feel; we may create stories in an attempt to relieve our fear or our pain. We might blame others or even strike out against a perceived enemy. The pain of unexamined, unresolved fear and anger is the source of much human distress. When we take the time to clear our minds, to find our center, to grieve, we often find a new perspective and begin to heal. (KBW)

A Blessing

Blessed are You, Eternal One,
who has provided me with such color and intensity in my
 emotional life.
I may be passionate, reflective, zealous, angry, fearful, joyful.
All this provides hues and textures to my experiences.
Help me recognize Your plan and Your teachings through my
 emotional responses,
and help me care for myself so I may enjoy emotional well-being.

Surrendering to Grief

Rabbi Anne Brener, LCSW

Y ou say that you don't recognize yourself? That you behave in ways that seem totally alien to you? You keep losing things or having outbursts of anger? You think that you are going crazy? Hearing this does not worry me. In fact, when one of my psychotherapy clients tells me that this is what is going on, I am often relieved. If this is true of you, it is likely to mean that your current difficulties are not the sign of a serious disorder that has been lurking for a lifetime. The fact that the behavior is so alien to you indicates that you are probably suffering a grief reaction or what my profession also calls a "situational" or "adjustment disorder." This is a direct reaction to a clear stress. It can be dealt with—*if* you are willing to risk opening yourself up.

This is not an easy thing to do. Suppressed emotion, stored near the surface, can be terrifying. Many fear that if the lid is taken off, the outpouring of tears or anger will never stop. But it is only the unfelt feelings that do not change. The pain or anger or whatever feeling is associated with the grief continues for a while, and then the bottom is reached, or things change, or a different emotion surfaces.

Avoiding your feelings means avoiding your own depth. It means avoiding the transforming experiences that life offers and failing to come to terms with your own personal history. Avoiding a feeling only prolongs it. Becoming familiar with the dimensions of the pain allows you to be less frightened and to cope more readily when the feeling comes up again. By overcoming the fear that suppresses the feelings, we become privy to the richness of our inner life.

Excerpted from *Mourning and Mitzvah, 2nd Edition: A Guided Journal for Walking the Mourner's Path through Grief to Healing* (Jewish Lights) by **Rabbi Anne Brener, LCSW**, professor of ritual and human development at the Academy for Jewish Religion in California.

Making the Choice to Heal

To say it simply: Our lives can teach us lessons. In this learning process, we have two choices: We can deny the learning and hold fast to our original vision of our self, the world, and the way "it ought to be." Or we can let our history be our teacher. It is this latter path that yields wisdom and understanding.

I have certainly had to struggle with this choice. This isn't what I had planned for my life. I would not have set out to become an expert on mourning. But this is the life that I was given.

There is a story about Reb Zusya, an eighteenth-century Hasidic master. Zusya said, "When God calls me, I will not be taken to account about why I was not a better Moses or a better Abraham. I will have to account for why I was not a better Zusya."

Like Zusya, I had a choice about whose life I would live. I could spend my life yearning for what might have been, railing against what was, or I could tell the truth about my life and use it as my teacher, taking every turn as a challenge for growth.

The difficulty in surrendering to process is that there is no road map. I can't tell you what you will experience along the way, or who you will be when you get there. I can tell you that it isn't going to be easy, that it may get worse before it gets better, and that the alternatives to taking this journey are worse than the journey itself. These alternatives may include depression, prolonged numbness, decreased satisfaction with your remaining relationships, addiction, emotional difficulties that manifest as physical symptoms, or significantly less zest for living.

Do these sound like satisfactory alternatives to facing the feelings of loss? If you are open enough to have read this far, they probably do not.

I'll say it once more. The one thing that I do know with certainty from my own struggles and from being midwife to countless others as they face their dark sides: Feelings that find expression change. And *that* change is the process that brings transformation....

The first thing to do is to stop holding your breath and counting the minutes until your pain is over. Mourning will end only by taking long breaths that help to deepen your focus on whatever you feel at any one time. This is the great paradox of the mourning process.

Whatever the timetable, feelings do change. The mourning process works, if you will engage in it. Fully engaging in mourning means that you will be a different person from the one you were before you began.

Practice: Beginning the Process

Now, take a slow, deep breath. This is where our work begins. With this breath, we will go on to create your *mekom hanekhama*—your place of comfort—your place for telling the truth. What did you feel when you read the above sentence, "Fully engaging in mourning means that you will be a different person from the one you were before you began"? Respond honestly. Did you feel hopeful? Or did you feel a clutching in the pit of your stomach? While some people may feel almost giddy at the promise of relief, others are horrified at the thought that they could ever accept a world devoid of the person they have lost. Tell yourself your reaction to the promise of change.

There are no right or wrong answers to the above question. In fact, today's answer may be very different from the one you might give to the same question tomorrow or in a week. That's the nature of any process—change. Therefore, our goal in raising the issues in this exercise is not to seek some immutable truth, but to create a path for *hesped* [eulogy]—a place where you can seek an honest and full expression of your feelings.

A Prayer for Prayer

Rabbi Sheldon Zimmerman

O My God
My soul's companion
My heart's precious friend
I turn to You.

I need to close out the noise
To rise above the noise
The noise that interrupts—
The noise that separates—
The noise that isolates.
I need to hear You again.

In the silence of my innermost being,
In the fragments of my yearned-for wholeness,
I hear whispers of Your presence—
Echoes of the past when You were with me
When I felt Your nearness
When together we walked—
When You held me close, embraced me in Your love,
laughed with me in my joy.
I yearn to hear You again.

In Your oneness, I find healing.
In the promise of Your love, I am soothed.
In Your wholeness, I too can become whole again.

Excerpted from *Healing of Soul, Healing of Body: Spiritual Leaders Unfold the Strength and Solace in Psalms* (Jewish Lights), edited by Rabbi Simkha Y. Weintraub, CSW. **Rabbi Sheldon Zimmerman** is a past president of the Central Conference of American Rabbis and Hebrew Union College–Jewish Institute of Religion, and is currently rabbi at the Jewish Center of the Hamptons.

Please listen to my call—
help me find the words
help me find the strength within
help me shape my mouth, my voice, my heart
so that I can direct my spirit and find You in prayer
In words only my heart can speak
In songs only my soul can sing
Lifting my eyes and heart to You.

Adonai S'fatai Tiftach—open my lips, precious God,
so that I can speak with You again.

Finding Our Center

Rabbi Lori Forman-Jacobi

An ignorant person believes that the whole universe exists only for him.... If, therefore, anything happens contrary to his expectations he at once concludes that the whole universe is evil.

Moses Maimonides

Children believe the world revolves around them. This is the nature of childhood. However, as we mature, hopefully we learn that this is far from true. Otherwise we run the risk of becoming overly self-centered, an alienating trait if ever there was one. We learn that our concerns, worries, and anxieties cannot always take center stage. Of course, we may know people who have never realized this important truth. They talk incessantly about themselves. They still blame the whole world if things do not go the way they expect.

If we find ourselves finding fault with the whole world, our entire community, or our family members, let us step back and take a "reality check." For the reality is, life fulfills some of our expectations and not others; that's just the way it goes. We struggle to stay on our spiritual path and be in relationship with God even when we are deeply disappointed or aggrieved. It takes faith to keep our place in the world in perspective and not cast blame blindly.

Excerpted from *Restful Reflections: Nighttime Inspiration to Calm the Soul, Based on Jewish Wisdom* (Jewish Lights) by Rabbi Kerry Olitzky and **Rabbi Lori Forman-Jacobi**, director of the Jewish Journey Project, a revolutionary educational initiative for children in grades 3 to 8.

No Guarantees

Rabbi Edwin Goldberg, DHL

We know, of course, that no one alive is free of such suffering and disappointment. It is part and parcel of the human condition. Most of us recognize this sad truth and have even come to terms with a tolerable level of sadness. Yet there are still certain disappointments that challenge the very foundations of our life. I speak not only of great personal tragedies, such as the loss of a child. I also refer to relatively small setbacks that lead us to question everything we hold dear in life. The underlying principle of such disappointments is that they are completely unexpected. They are things that we never thought we would have to worry about.

We might call these "unspoken promises." These are the goals and enjoyments in life we assume are ours to expect, almost as a right of being alive. In our expectations we are like the Israelite farmer described by the prophet Isaiah. The farmer carefully planted his vines, built a watchtower for fortification, and had a winepress hewn out of stone. Then he waited for good grapes, but wild grapes grew instead. So the farmer cries out, "What else can I do to my vineyard that I did not do? Why did I hope for good grapes but receive wild ones?" He had done everything right, but the loss still was his to bear. The unspoken promise that his hard work would be rewarded was not fulfilled....

Every time we feel that life should be fair, we are reflecting an unspoken promise. Every time we think we should be rewarded for being good, or expect that life will have a happy ending if we try our best, we are being just like the Israelite farmer. Whenever we do everything right and expect happiness in return, we are hoping the world will keep its unspoken promise to us.

Excerpted from *Saying No and Letting Go: Jewish Wisdom on Making Room for What Matters Most* (Jewish Lights) by **Rabbi Edwin Goldberg, DHL**, senior rabbi at Temple Sholom in Chicago.

No More Pretending

Such beliefs will never lead to happiness or even contentment of any kind. Instead, we must surrender such expectations if we want to find peace of mind. This begins with considering anew the unspoken promises that fill our lives and that may lead to bitterness and disappointment. We should ask ourselves: What unspoken promises are we counting on to come true? And how will we respond to life if they should not be fulfilled? Will our disappointment lead to doubt, or can we turn our loss into a richer life, filled with renewed faith? Can we accept that life gives us no guarantees and still find joy in our days? Can we turn our suffering into serenity?

When it comes to unspoken promises, the first thing to do is to bring them to the surface, to make the hidden revealed. In order to be aware of our unspoken promises, we need to confront some painful possibilities that we would rather ignore. As Ralph Waldo Emerson once observed, "Life invests itself with inevitable conditions, which the unwise seek to dodge." We would like to be exempt from these inevitable conditions or at least pretend that they won't happen for a very long time. We may also accept these conditions intellectually, but accepting them emotionally is another matter entirely....

If we expect that any of these laws do not apply to us, we will be like the sixty-something woman who told me that, after losing her ninety-year-old father, she did not believe in God anymore. Although I understood her pain in losing her loved one, at the time her declaration of doubt made no sense to me. How could anyone not believe in God after losing a parent who had reached the fullness of years? Now I understand that her disappointment was more than grief over losing a beloved parent. An unspoken promise—that her father would always be there for her—had been broken. So she couldn't believe in God anymore. Or more precisely, she couldn't believe in a God who had promised that her father would live forever.

Life Promises Us Nothing

My message to this grieving woman, and to all of us, is to suggest that such unspoken promises lead us down the wrong path in life. To believe in such promises is to set the stage for toxic anger and resentment. Surely there must be another way.

Such a way would be to admit that our unspoken promises are not valid and binding. Indeed, perhaps this is the true message of the holiest declaration in Judaism on the holiest night of the year, *Kol Nidrei*: Life does not promise us anything. Life comes with no guarantees....

Such a realization means all of us should be more aware of the gifts we enjoy, even as we surrender our belief that such gifts cannot be taken away. Even as we say good-bye to the dreams we have for ourselves and our families that won't come true. Our disappointments will be real, but they can be placed into a sacred context of not taking anything or anyone for granted.

In such a sacred context, we can learn that the love we have for others doesn't stop just because our unspoken promises may be broken.

Praying in Hard Times

Rabbi Lawrence A. Hoffman, PhD

Prayer is an art form. It affirms our deepest suspicions of what really matters in ways that are undeniable. Artists tell truths that others dare not dream of. When science does that, it too becomes an art; even mathematical models are said to be "elegant." The inner life has its own breathtaking elegance. As prayer reaches in, not out, it transports us to our bravest imaginings of what we are.

Scientists understand the body. There, at least, the math works out: so much water, some potassium and other minerals, a multiplicity of specialized cells determined by a genetic code. But what of our yearning to be something more? To matter in the long run, though our life be pained or short? Do we pass on to posterity something beyond the genes that were passed on to us?

Especially when our body flags, we can't help but wonder if that is all there is. Through the art of prayer, we formulate beliefs about things that are utterly compelling even though no evidence is possible. Prayer convinces me, for instance, that I am more than the sum of my bodily cells, that disease and torment cannot touch the essence of who I am, and that my existence somehow goes on beyond the day of bodily death. I do not pray such things because I already believe them; I believe them because I have prayed them. At its heart, prayer is a venture into the unknown, taking us beyond all science to realms where there is not even any mathematics to work out. Is the universe friendly to us? Are we mere accidents of circumstance? Do we count for anything? After we are gone, where do we go? On ordinary days, we may not think much about such things. But in moments of sickness and grief, questions like these inevitably flood the mind....

Excerpted from *Praying in Hard Times*, a LifeLight™ pastoral care pamphlet (Jewish Lights), by **Rabbi Lawrence A. Hoffman, PhD**, author of over thirty books, world-renowned liturgist and holder of the Stephen and Barbara Friedman Chair in Liturgy, Worship and Ritual at Hebrew Union College–Jewish Institute of Religion in New York.

I have discovered three basic reasons to turn to prayer in times of trouble.

- *If we think we are victimized, we are*—but only by our own unreal and unhealthy imaginings. Prayer exchanges those imaginings for the view that the universe is not antagonistic to us: despite our pain, there is help and love beyond ourselves.

- *We are never without our own inner resources.* Prayer awakens us to the interior regions of our soul, to our real humanity that nothing can destroy, and to the certainty that we matter, eternally, no matter how much we suffer in the present.

- *Finally, praying for ourselves and for others helps us see that we are not alone.* Rather, we are linked to a network of love from which divine miracles really flow.

Releasing Yourself

My God, the soul you have given me is pure.

Morning Prayers

A broken spirit, who can bear?

Proverbs 18:14

You are not expected to sail perfectly through life, much less through the lashing waves of grief. You are not expected to have unswerving faith, unending patience, or bottomless compassion and forgiveness for others.

You may find yourself struggling with guilt and regret—but there is no need to add to your suffering by letting these take hold. Here are tools and encouragement for letting go of feelings of inadequacy, for forgiving yourself, your loved one, and friends and family who may have let you down in your time of grief. Let it go, find healing, make peace. Don't let regret, guilt, or resentment keep you bound.

Experiencing Your Pure Soul

Nan Fink Gefen, PhD

One of the Hebrew words for soul is *neshamah* (pronounced "neh-shah-mah"). The concept of soul is confusing for many of us. We can't locate our soul anywhere in our bodies nor can we point to its existence, so we wonder if it is real.

Yet we sense that there is something within us that is "pure" or uncontaminated. Despite our imperfections, despite all the times we've done harm, we know in our most reasonable moments that we're not entirely bad. Even the most destructive people throughout history have a core of goodness, although it is buried beneath their evil acts and exists only in potential form.

I like to lead students in a simple meditation that focuses on the words, *Elohai, neshamah shenatata be, t'horah he* (pronounced "el-oh-high, neh-shah-mah sh-nah-tah-tah bee, tay-hor-ah hee"). Or in English, "My God, the soul You have given me is pure." Those who are comfortable with Hebrew can use the Hebrew words, but it works just as well in English.

This meditation is especially helpful for people who have lost sight of their own goodness and who dwell on their imperfections. Once they experience the soul within as an undeniable reality, they more easily let go of the self-inflated idea of their own insignificance.

The words for this meditation come from the early part of the morning service. The prayer says, "My God, the soul You have given me is pure. You formed it, You breathed it into me, and You preserve it within me. You will take my soul from me, but You will restore it in the time to come." Thus we

---

Excerpted from *Discovering Jewish Meditation*, 2nd Edition: *Instruction and Guidance for Learning an Ancient Spiritual Practice* (Jewish Lights) by **Nan Fink Gefen, PhD**, cofounder of *Tikkun* magazine and the meditation center Chochmat HaLev in Berkeley, California.

see soul as hosted by us, but not owned by us. We do not create it, because it already exists.

According to the Jewish mystical tradition, five aspects of soul dwell within each of us. They are related to each other, but have different characteristics. The first of these, *nefesh*, is the soul that is given to us at birth and that leaves us when we die. It's the most tangible, earthly aspect of soul. Next comes *ruach*, which exists on the level of deep understanding. It's that part within us that makes intuitive leaps. The third aspect of soul is *neshamah*. Here we find the spark of the Divine revealed most strongly. The final two aspects are beyond anything we can know or sense, because they are so much a part of the Divine. Thus they are hardly mentioned.

Soul exists in all of us, but it is bound and hidden by our negative traits. For some people it is hardly present. But as we do our self-refinement and take responsibility for our self-destructive, harmful ways, the soul within us becomes more and more revealed. Over time, then, we become more "soulful," and able to relate to others and to God in deeper ways.

The *kavannah* (intention) of the *neshamah* meditation is to experience the soul within.

Practice: *Neshamah* Meditation

Make yourself comfortable, then breathe deeply, making a sound with your exhalation. Do this several times, letting go of the tension within you.

Let your breath settle into its usual rhythm.

Observe it for a few minutes.

When your mind has quieted down, you are ready to begin.

Focus on the words, "My God, the soul You have given me is pure."

Or *Elohai, neshamah shenatata be, t'horah he.*

Say the words silently to yourself over and over.

Say them with each breath.

With each breath, receive the soul.

Experience the soul.

Know the soul.

Feel the connection with God,

The source of soul,

The provider of soul.

If your mind wanders, observe where it went and bring it back to the meditation.

If a noise or movement distracts you, let it go.

"My God, the soul You have given me is pure."

Elohai, neshamah shenatata be, t'horah he.

Letting Go of Self-Accusation

Rabbi Harold M. Schulweis

How is the light of God revealed? God is found in life and in serious conversation. To find God, we must enter into a dialogue with our *tzelem*, the image of God that lodges within us and contains the potential for wisdom, sanity, morality, and healing. This dialogue with the *tzelem*, with the God within, is called "prayer" (in Hebrew, it is called *tefillah*). Prayer can be an internal debate. It sometimes feels as if we are wrestling with ourselves....

How can I break the grip of this relentless self-accusation and relieve myself of this heavy weight? The *tzelem* counsels, "Separate the threads that have been so entangled and knotted that they seem unbreakable." The *tzelem* proffers a line from the prophet Isaiah: "Precept by precept, precept by precept, line by line, line by line, here a little, there a little." This mantra of wisdom calms my fear. I do not have to do everything at once. The *tzelem* urges me to remember, "This is not your first anxiety. Remember what happened to you before. You overcame that yesterday and before that as well."

The *tzelem* understands my compulsion to stamp labels on myself: "I am lazy. I am slow. I am friendless. I am foolish. I am impulsive. I am a failure. I always mess up." The *tzelem* points out how in negativity I am drawn to totalitarian words like "always" or "never" or "everyone" or "no one."

The *tzelem* counsels me, "Remember the Exodus. Do not say that you have never enjoyed freedom and liberation and hope. Remember the journey of your people from slavery to freedom, from sorrow to joy, from mourning to festivity, from darkness to light, from bondage to redemption." There is an attitude toward life that informs the way a life is lived. It is not an accident

Excerpted from *Bringing Your Sadness to God*, a LifeLight™ pastoral care pamphlet (Jewish Lights) by **Rabbi Harold M. Schulweis**, one of the most respected spiritual leaders and teachers of his generation. Rabbi Schulweis's other books include *Conscience: The Duty to Obey and the Duty to Disobey* (also Jewish Lights).

that the opening chapter of the Book of Genesis concludes that "God saw everything that He had made and it was very good."

The Hafetz Hayim (a nineteenth-century rabbi and writer on ethics) commented, "Despair not. It is darkest before the dawn. Before light was created, all was darkness on the face of the deep."

The Great Silence of Doubt

Rabbi James L. Mirel and Karen Bonnell Werth

One of the great gifts of the Jewish tradition is the permission to have moments of doubt and questions of faith. A Jew is weighed on the scale of action and not on the scale of faith. The great midrashic wish of the Holy One—"O that they might forsake Me and keep My commandments"—captures this reality perfectly.

Doubt is the state of mind that is the necessary companion of faith. It is twofold. Doubt can be the thought—however fleeting—that there is no God and nothing of ultimate meaning in our lives. The biblical philosopher called Kohelet stated this poignantly when he wrote in Ecclesiastes 1:2, "Vanity of vanities, all is vanity." The other kind of doubt is that while there *is* a God, somehow that God cares nothing about us or is even antagonistic toward us. The psalmist in agony cries out, "My God, my God, why have You forsaken me?" (Psalm 22:2). Both of these varieties of doubt depress us, yet there is also something comforting in a tradition that teaches that God accepts the shortcomings of our faith.

When we feel abandoned, unprotected, uncared for by God, we may feel painfully alone. As it is written in Lamentations (3:17–18), "My soul is bereft of peace, I have forgotten what happiness is; so I say, 'Gone is my strength and my hope from the Eternal One.'" Doubt, disconnection, spiritual despair—this is a loneliness so penetrating it can leave a person with an unbearable sense of insignificance. As we question the meaning of life and the purpose of suffering, we struggle to make sense out of the darkness.

It is hoped that these times of spiritual despair or doubt are merely valleys in lives of faith and security. But, when despair arises, we can be comforted

Excerpted from *Stepping Stones to Jewish Spiritual Living: Walking the Path Morning, Noon, and Night* (Jewish Lights) by **Rabbi James L. Mirel**, rabbi emeritus of Temple B'nai Torah in Bellevue, Washington, and **Karen Bonnell Werth**, a health-care professional and developer of the yearlong facilitator training program for the Compassionate Listening Project.

by knowing that there is no faith in the human condition without the great silence of doubt.

Prayer for Doubt

My God, my God, why have You forsaken me?
In my time of need, I feel so alone. I want to reach out to Someone or Something beyond myself, but at this moment I cannot.
Help me believe in You.
I need to feel that this universe is not cold and unfeeling.
I need to sense that my pain is for some higher purpose.
Speak to me, O Hidden One.
Answer my prayers even if I speak them with skepticism.
Touch me—just a little bit—and then I will be able to overcome
    my doubts and embrace You in love and in hope.
Reach out to me and I will reach out to You.

The Pain of Spiritual Doubt and Guilt

The whole community broke into loud cries, and the people wept that night. All the Israelites railed against Moses and Aaron. "If only we had died in the land of Egypt, if only we might die in this wilderness." ... And they said to one another, "Let us head back for Egypt."

Numbers 14:1–2, 4

We read this painful account of "losing faith." As the enemy surrounded them, our ancient people feared that their future would be worse than slavery. They were frightened to the point of giving up their freedom, their faith in God's goodness, their faith in themselves, and their own confidence that they would persevere and that God would be with them.

May we be gentle with ourselves when we lose faith and be comforted by the fact that we are in the good company of our ancestors—and that like them, we will prevail and experience what it means to be "children of the Eternal One our God" (Deuteronomy 14:1). May we be confident that the sun will rise with the dawn, and that we are not alone, even though we may not understand why or how solutions will unfold in the dark of night. *This* is called "having faith."

Healing to the Point
of Forgiving

Rabbi Elie Kaplan Spitz
with Erica Shapiro Taylor

A story of forgiveness that has had a great impact on me was told to me by a congregant about her father's death. The daughter, a nurse, had come to me and asked for guidance in offering a caring presence at her father's deathbed, given her father's past cruelty to her mother. I offered her the wisdom of Rebbe Nachman that she seek out a single good point in her father, a characteristic that reflected the spark of the Divine within him, even if it had not been fully realized. I suggested that she consider his own despair at his flaws, failings, and shattered state and in the end, I asked her to embrace him with compassion. A week later she called me from her father's deathbed: "I am sitting here holding my father's hand. He just died. And I was able to be fully and compassionately present for him. I found points of goodness in him, qualities that reflected God's image. And when I said to him, 'It's okay, you can go now,' he did, he died within moments."

Healing fully requires we realize our capacity to forgive others and ourselves. Whether we are caught in the spiral of deep despair that fills us with self-loathing or are overwhelmed by resentment and bitterness directed toward others, to forgive is to let go of much of the anger that we hold on to. Anger is like a torch we cling to only to find that the flame has burned us. To be able to forgive is to move from anger to acceptance. To forgive is to acknowledge that we have shortcomings and yet are worthy of love. From

Excerpted from *Healing from Despair: Choosing Wholeness in a Broken World* (Jewish Lights) by Rabbi Elie Kaplan Spitz with Erica Shapiro Taylor. **Rabbi Elie Kaplan Spitz** is a spiritual leader and scholar specializing in topics of spirituality and Judaism, and rabbi of Congregation B'nai Israel in Tustin, California. His other books include *Does the Soul Survive? A Jewish Journey to Belief in Afterlife, Past Lives and Living with Purpose* (also Jewish Lights).

that place of humility we remember that we all are capable of committing wrongs. And yet that fragility is part of what it means to be human.

Practice: Tools for Healing

Rebbe Nachman's Points

Bring to mind a person who has done you wrong. Examine his or her deeds and identify just one act that evidences goodness. Search and find another point of goodness and then another. Connect the dots, revealing an image of goodness. Put into perspective the wrong done within the larger tapestry of the wrong-doer's life. Allow yourself to forgive by embracing the wholeness of the other.

Forgive Yourself

Examine yourself and find an act or attitude of goodness. Do not be too quick to dismiss your deed as prompted by selfish motives. Examine within the deed, finding a point of goodness. Continue reviewing your deeds, finding another and still another point of goodness. Connect the dots and allow yourself to value your foundational goodness. Make a commitment to more consistently act with goodness and with more selfless motives in the future.

Tikkun: Healing the Dead

Rabbi David A. Cooper

Raba was sitting near the bed of Rav Nachman when he [Nachman] was in his last breaths of life. Rav Nachman said to Raba, "Please urge [the angel of death] not to cause me any pain." Raba replied, "Are you not yourself a friend [of the angel of death, and therefore could ask him yourself]?" Nachman replied, "Who can contend at such a time as this?" Raba then requested, "[After you are on the other side] please let your soul appear before me [when I am dreaming, so that I can discover something of your passage]." [After the death of Nachman, his soul appeared to Raba in a dream.] When it appeared, Raba asked: "Did you have any pain [in the transition]?" Nachman answered: "It was as easy as removing a hair from milk."

Babylonian Talmud, *Mo'ed Katan* 28a

This visualization of healing the dead is unique in that we are able to not only work on our own spiritual development, but we can also influence, in kabbalistic terms, soul forces that have passed over into other realms. This has profound kabbalistic content in the sense that we can work with energy on an entirely different level of existence. This meditation is based on the idea that time is relative and that even though a soul force may have passed into the other realm, we can still influence it from this realm of reality. Indeed, the primary advantage of being alive in this world is having free will. This being

Excerpted from *The Handbook of Jewish Meditation Practices: A Guide for Enriching the Sabbath and Other Days of Your Life* (Jewish Lights) by **Rabbi David A. Cooper**, retreat leader, spiritual teacher, and award-winning author of many books, including *Three Gates to Meditation Practice: A Personal Journey in Sufism, Buddhism and Judaism* (also Jewish Lights).

so, we can accomplish some things in this reality of existence with our free will that soul forces cannot achieve in realms that lack free will.

Practice: Repairing the Soul

Let your imagination flow with this. You will discover it to be a useful and significant meditation that will cause healing on many different levels, and you will find that it will bring a new realization in terms of your relationship with someone who has left this world.

1. Begin by sitting relaxed, eyes closed, breathing normally. Do this for at least five minutes.

2. Bring into your imagination someone who is deceased. It can be a close friend or a relative; it can be someone who passed away recently or long ago. The important thing is that it should be someone you personally knew when he or she was alive. Bring this image into your imagination, remembering the person.

3. Notice your emotions. Notice if you are feeling sad. Now allow yourself to rise above your emotions so that you can enter into an objective frame of mind, a place of equanimity. Imagine your soul and the soul of the deceased one are having a conversation, and let the one who is deceased tell you, briefly, what it feels it accomplished when it was alive. Do this for a few minutes.

4. Now let the other soul tell you what it feels it failed to accomplish. Let it tell you what its shortcomings were when it was alive. Do this for a few minutes.

5. Imagine saying to this soul, "If there were one thing that could be done at this time, one fixing that could be made for something you failed to do when you were alive, what would that one thing be? What would you change about your life, if you could?" Listen carefully to what this soul tells you.

6. Now, using the full range of your imagination, imagine that you are doing the very thing that this soul tells you it needs to do. Do this for the soul. That is, imagine what it would have been like for this person when he or she was alive, had this one thing been done. Once you are able to envision this in your mind, replay it over and over again, with as many variations on a theme as you need in order to make this image complete. In other words, you are recasting your memory of this soul in a way that

imagines the person to be who you believe he or she would have wanted to be. Do this for at least five minutes.

7. Notice your emotions and your breath. If you are feeling your emotions and you are breathing differently, your imagination is deeply engaged. Now come back to the balanced breath. Let go of all the images. Observe the chest rising and falling. Take two deep breaths and open your eyes.

You can repeat this process a few times with this soul, but it is not recommended to continue for too long or to return to the same soul too often. This *tikkun* (fixing) is accomplished quickly and one can feel free to move on without dwelling more than the amount of time designated above. Thus, do not repeat this exercise more than a couple of times a month, at the most.

This is a highly recommended meditation, especially for people who have recently lost loved ones. It has a powerful impact on your soul and on the soul of your loved one. We can do things in this world, we can actually continue the process of the *tikkun*, the fixing, that the departed soul set out to do.

Remembering and Letting Go

Rabbi Nancy Fuchs-Kreimer, PhD, and Rabbi Nancy H. Wiener, DMin

"There is a land of the living and a land of the dead," wrote Thornton Wilder. During *Yizkor*, the memorial service on Yom Kippur day, the border between those two lands is more open than usual. Three other times during the year *Yizkor* is said to memorialize parents, siblings, partners, and children, but *Yizkor* on Yom Kippur is particularly intense. Thinking about those we have lost is especially challenging at a time of soul-searching and moral accounting.

Death ends lives, but not relationships. In remembering those who are gone, we can't help but remember our unfinished business with them. Sometimes we realize that something is holding us back in our relationship, even though it has nothing directly to do with our partner. It may be that we need to be forgiven by someone who is no longer alive. Or we need to forgive someone but cannot, since they have died. We know that we will not be able to fully be the partner we want to be until we have dealt with this old business. Yom Kippur is an excellent time to address those things that seem beyond our ability to fix. "The most unnoticed of all miracles is the miracle of repentance," wrote Abraham Joshua Heschel. "It is not the same thing as rebirth; it is transformation, creation. In the dimension of time, there is no going back. But the

Excerpted from *Judaism for Two: A Spiritual Guide for Strengthening and Celebrating Your Loving Relationship* (Jewish Lights) by **Rabbi Nancy Fuchs-Kreimer, PhD**, director of the department of multifaith studies and initiatives and associate professor of religious studies at Reconstructionist Rabbinical College, and **Rabbi Nancy H. Wiener, DMin**, clinical director of the Jacob and Hilda Blaustein Center for Pastoral Counseling at Hebrew Union College–Jewish Institute of Religion. Rabbi Fuchs-Kreimer is also a contributor to *Broken Tablets: Restoring the Ten Commandments and Ourselves* (also Jewish Lights), edited by Rachel S. Mikva.

power of repentance causes time to be created backward and allows recreation of the past to take place." On what level can we believe that?

Deborah, recently married for a second time, had been divorced many years before. She had often thought—especially during Yom Kippur—of trying to get together with her ex-husband to talk through old wounds. She knew there were things she would do differently if she had them to do again. Although she had reached the point where she felt ready to tell her ex and ask his forgiveness, she never actually had. When he died—quite suddenly—she found herself mourning both the lost opportunities of her first marriage and the chance to make amends. She explained to her new husband that this year *Yizkor* would be a time when she would have to be alone. She had work to do.

What if we cannot let go of our own anger? Holding a grudge, it is said, is like giving up space in your soul without receiving rent. What a burden we impose on ourselves! A young man once turned to a wise teacher for help with an anger he could not shake. The teacher told him that he had to carry a brick around with him wherever he went for a week. At the end of the week, he was exhausted. "Let it go," the teacher said. "It is a heavy load for you. Just let it go."

Yom Kippur helps us find a place of surrender where we will be able to lay down our anger or disappointments and move forward. It provides a statute of limitations on resentment. If the past can be remade only by the miracle of repentance, the future can still be created by our own efforts.

Saying No

Rabbi Naomi Levy

How do we regain our focus? How do we reclaim balance? How do we make room for rest? ... Gathering ourselves up can transform us from a diluted self to a state of concentration and focus and truth. Through contraction we make room—for others, for God, for miracles, and for surprise. By contracting we actually grow. We learn to hear what others are really trying to say to us, we learn to hear the voice of our own souls, and we learn to hear the voice of God calling out to us.

The word "no" can be quite difficult to utter, but it is the key to a life of boundaries. We must learn how to use it with others, but also how to say it to ourselves. Wanting more can lead us down a path to misery and envy. How else is it possible that we can have so much and still feel so empty?

Set limits, pull back, set aside time for rest, move from chaos to focus, say no, listen to what you've been ignoring, make room for what you've been longing for and you will uncover the true meaning of the word "full." A whole life is waiting for you.

Excerpted from the foreword to *Saying No and Letting Go: Jewish Wisdom on Making Room for What Matters Most* (Jewish Lights) by Rabbi Edwin Goldberg, DHL. **Rabbi Naomi Levy** is spiritual leader of Nashuva in Los Angeles and author of *Hope Will Find You*, *Talking to God*, and *To Begin Again*.

Lingering Grief

Rabbi David Lyon

Sometimes [underground] mourning can resurface when we become reflective about our life. When it does reappear and our sadness emerges again, one expert, Bruce Horacek, calls it "shadow grief." He describes it as

> a dull ache in the background of one's feelings that remains fairly constant and that, under certain circumstances and on certain occasions, comes bubbling to the surface, sometimes in the form of tears, sometimes not, but always accompanied by a feeling of sadness and mild sense of anxiety.[1]

What do we do to mitigate our shadow grief? A part of the answer lies in each of us. It is found in the pure soul God created in us, which remains tied to its Creator. Another source of comfort is the memory of the very people with whom we shared life-changing experiences. These memories become powerful reminders of what will always be important to us. The people we miss were those we counted on, learned from, and continue to love deeply. Yet another answer about how to mitigate shadow grief is found in a Rabbinic tale:

> The son of a rabbi mourned the death of his beloved father. Day after day, the son went to the cemetery and threw himself on the grave of his father. One day as the son gave way to fits of sorrow, his father appeared to him in a vision. His father said to him, "My son, do you think that you honor my memory with your grief? Offer me no tributes of tears. Build for me no monuments of sorrow. Do not weep for me. Live for me!

Excerpted from *God of Me: Imagining God throughout Your Lifetime* (Jewish Lights) by **Rabbi David Lyon**, senior rabbi at Congregation Beth Israel in Houston, Texas, and chairman of the board of the Institute for Spirituality and Health at Texas Medical Center.

"Show your love by obedience to God's commandments, by devotion to faith, and by service to your fellow human beings. This," said his father, "is the memorial that truly honors the departed." After hearing these words, the son lifted himself from his father's grave, and went forth to make of his father's memory a perpetual light to guide him on paths of righteousness and truth.[2]

The rabbi gave his son a gift when he told him to keep living by honoring his father's memory through his deeds. We can assume that the son left the cemetery to pursue life and to bring honor to his father by doing so. We, too, must fulfill the meaning of our life, enriched by the memories of those who have died. Our shadow grief may linger for years, but we cannot allow it to become a stumbling block to our life. Those who remember their loved ones do so with pictures they see in their home, with a memorial plaque in temple, and with regular contributions of time or resources that help others know how his or her memory still inspires us to do and be our best. All is not lost if we regard memory as the sacred gift that it is.

God's comfort can also help take away the sting of our loss. Our loved ones provided us so much, but we were not completely dependent on them. Our life was full because of their contributions of emotional and other forms of support, but it was also full because of what we contributed to those relationships, friendships, and special bonds.

In an anonymous poem, the writer suggests that while we grow and live as children of our parents and in other loving relationships, we sometimes fail to see what they tried to give us, so that now, in their absence, we can forget what we gained and which endures beyond their lifetime. The poem, composed in both English and Yiddish, is called "All I Got Was Words":

When I was young and fancy free,
My folks had no fine clothes for me;
All I got was words:
   Got tzu danken (Thank God)
   Got vet geben (God will provide)
   Zol mir leben un zein gezunt (Live and be well)
When I was wont to travel far,
They didn't provide me with a car;
All I got was words:
   Geh gezunt (Be healthy)

Geh pamelech (Go slowly)
Hub a glickliche reise (Have a good life)
I wanted to increase my knowledge,
But they couldn't send me to college;
All I got was words:
Hub saychel (Have common sense)
Zei nischt kein narr (You are not a fool)
Torah iz di beste schorah (Torah is the best lesson)
The years have flown—the world has turned,
Things I've gotten; things I've learned;
Yet I remember:
Zog dem emes (Tell the truth)
Gib tzedakah (Give charity)
Hub rachmonas (Have compassion)
Zei a mentsh! (Be a mensch, a good person)
All I got was words.[3]

The Yiddish words, which are not translated in the original poem, were aphorisms that were meant to be part of a rich inheritance of ideas. The poet's parents didn't have "things" to leave him; they had ideas and dreams. The poet laments that all he got was words. But we know that what he got was far more important. He knew that his parents wanted the best for him in whatever he chose for himself in his lifetime. All they really wanted for him was expressed in the words *Zei a mentsh!* "Be a mensch!" (an exceptionally fine human being).

Surely, our own inheritance cannot be reduced to material objects or money. It is also the lessons, the words, and the experiences of our lives. Perhaps not all of them are clear and understandable, but looking back, we can raise our estimation of our loved ones when we try to see clearly now what we could not necessarily see then. Now, looking back, we see their reasons, their methods, and even their madness. When they didn't seem to give love easily, they meant well anyway; when they didn't give us the things we wanted, they gave us what they thought we needed instead. When we acknowledge their absence, we know that they are more than a memory; they are part of who we are today and who we are still on the way to becoming.

The Angel of Losses

Rabbi Sandy Eisenberg Sasso

Jewish folklore tells of an angel of losses called Yode'a.[1] That angel and his servants spend all their time looking for losses. They search with a light. That light is nothing more than a small candle flame. They look inside the places of unbroken darkness to find what has vanished, and they keep in memory all that has been lost.

That is what we do when we recite memorial prayers. At home before the Yom Kippur fast we kindle a small twenty-four-hour candle, whose light we carry with us in our mind's eye to the synagogue, where more memorial lamps have already been lit. We wed those lights to the one we brought with us and then weave them all together with the *Yizkor* prayers we say, letting image and word illumine the unbroken darkness of the grave. Through that light of memory, we recall once again what we have lost. We recognize how deeply we carry our loved ones inside us, literally within our minds and our hearts. At that moment, we know that this is true. That is why the angel is given the name Yode'a, from the Hebrew word meaning "to know."

We are all servants of this angel of losses, who struggle in the places of deepest darkness, in the valley of shadows, to recover those losses and to rekindle within ourselves the glow of the souls of those who have died, for it becomes clear to us how we have been changed and what parts of ourselves are from our loved ones. We then know what we otherwise sometimes forget: that they are with us still. And we promise to live out the best that they have bequeathed to us.

That is how I understand the beautiful words of *El Malei Rachamim*:

Excerpted from *May God Remember: Memory and Memorializing in Judaism—Yizkor* in the *Prayers of Awe* series (Jewish Lights), edited by Rabbi Lawrence A. Hoffman, PhD. **Rabbi Sandy Eisenberg Sasso**, a parent, spiritual leader, and storyteller, is the award-winning author of many inspiring books, including *God's Paintbrush* and *In God's Name* (both Jewish Lights).

O God, full of compassion, Eternal Spirit of the Universe, grant perfect rest under the wings of Your presence to our loved one who has entered eternity. Compassionate One, hide him/her in the secret embrace of Your wings for all time. Bind his/her soul in the bond of eternal life.

Perhaps it is Yode'a, the angel of losses, guardian of memory, under whose wings our loved ones are hidden. They are carried in those secret places of our brains, inextricably bound up with us in the bond of life.

Courage in the Darkness

I have forgotten what happiness is.

Lamentations 3:17

Surely the darkness will hide me.

Psalm 139:11

What can you do when the darkness of grief and sorrow seem as if they will overwhelm you?

Keep doing the simple things you know to do. Know that God is present no matter how it feels. Sing—even if your song is more a groan than a melody. Let your heart expand as you resolve to keep loving in spite of uncertainty. Remind yourself of the reality of joy. Be patient with yourself. Keep wrestling with God and demand a blessing. Know that dawn is coming.

In the depths of darkness, may you gather your courage and seek out the hidden sparks in yourself and others.

The Echo of Your Promise

Rabbi Harold M. Schulweis

When I cry my voice trembles with fear
When I call out it cracks with anger.

How can I greet the dawn with song
when darkness eclipses the rising sun

To whom shall I turn
when the clouds of the present eclipse the rays of tomorrow

Turn me around to yesterday
that I may be consoled by its memories.

Were not the seas split asunder
did we not once walk together through the waters to the dry side

Did we not bless the
bread that came forth from the heavens

Did your voice not reach my ears
and direct my wanderings

The waters, the lightning, the thunder
remind me of yesterday's triumphs

Let the past offer proof of tomorrow
let it be my comforter and guarantor.

Excerpted from *Healing of Soul, Healing of Body: Spiritual Leaders Unfold the Strength and Solace in Psalms* (Jewish Lights), edited by Rabbi Simkha Y. Weintraub, CSW. **Rabbi Harold M. Schulweis** was one of the most respected spiritual leaders and teachers of his generation. Rabbi Schulweis's other books include *Conscience: The Duty to Obey and the Duty to Disobey* (also Jewish Lights).

I have been here before
known the fright and found your companionship.

I enter the sanctuary again
to await the echo of your promise.[1]

Crying Out for the Light

Rabbi Arthur Green, PhD

When God said, "Let there be light!" on Creation's first day, we are told, the light that came forth was too bright for God's creatures to bear. With it, a person could see "from one end of the world to the other." Such great light, revealing all the secret places of existence, would not allow for life as we know it. We creatures, human and animal alike, need to hide in order to exist. The light itself was thus set aside, so that we might be able to hide. Only "in the future that is coming" will such hiding no longer be needed.... If humanity is to exist and we are to remain human, the light must remain hidden.

But that same humanity desperately needs a bit of light. We cry out for guidance, for some sense that we are walking in the right direction. Human life is impossible without hope, and hope requires that something of the light be revealed. How do we call upon the light to guide us, to lead us in our own search for the truth that it bears within it? The hiding of the primal light, necessary as it might be for our very existence, at the same time appears to us as cruelty, a needless inflicting of pain upon this human creature condemned to seek meaning.

To that same one who is the source of our hope, the glimmer of light beyond the darkness, we protest the pain of living. We cry out in our hurt and our anger. We understand the need for the light's hiding, and yet we protest it. Surely there is no need for as much darkness as we have known! Yes, we have to experience emptiness in order to stretch and grow in spirit. We need to know the absence of light in order to strive forward in our human struggle. But could we not learn these without the deaths of so many million

---

Excerpted from *Seek My Face: A Jewish Mystical Theology* (Jewish Lights) by **Rabbi Arthur Green, PhD**, one of the world's preeminent authorities on Jewish thought and spirituality. Rabbi Green is Irving Brudnick Professor of Philosophy and Religion at Hebrew College and rector and founder of the Rabbinical School. Rabbi Green's other books include *Judaism's Ten Best Ideas: A Brief Guide for Seekers* (also Jewish Lights).

children? Could the path to understanding not be strewn with fewer victims, fewer human lives destroyed and abandoned of hope along the way? Every one of those human beings is an image of Y-H-W-H! Each time one of them gives up on life, the divine light grows dimmer. If we care about the diminishing of God's image in our world, we have to cry out.

True encounter with Oneness is given to us only in fleeting moments, glimpses quickly forgotten, as we rush onward with our daily lives. In their absence—what seems to us as "the absence of God" or the "hiding of God's face"—religious life becomes an act of defiance. Our faith becomes a rejection of absurdity, a refusal to accept emptiness as our final lot in life. Faith is our testimony—all evidence to the contrary notwithstanding—that the light still burns, that meaning is still to be found. We do not *deny* the absurdity of life. No human being, and especially no Jew, living in our times, could do that. We have seen the arbitrariness of fate, the depths of human cruelty, the indifference of both man and nature. We do not deny absurdity, but we reject it, we *defy* it. We stare into the face of darkness and proclaim that light still exists. We refuse to give in to hopelessness. The struggle for faith and the refusal to give in to despair are one and the same.

Confronting reality as fully as anyone who lives in our world, we know that there is another side to reality as well. The absence of God and the rule of darkness certainly represent a truth, one we do not deny. But we know a deeper truth as well. Here we are sustained by memory. The glow of those moments in which we glimpsed God's light still warms us. We Jews know, and sometimes still feel, the warmth of that glow from Sinai. The fire of God's mountain still burns, we proclaim, encircling and warming those who study Torah. But really that light burns in every person, the memory of those moments in our lives that were closest to true freedom, to understanding, and thus to fulfillment. These are "the Sea" and "Sinai" in our individual lives, the moments that inspire us and keep us on course in our journey.

The light within us needs to be rekindled, needs to have its glow restored. This usually comes about when we see a glimpse of that same light shining in another. That other may be a *tzaddik*—a righteous one whose light shines with a special brightness—or perhaps just an ordinary person, like the one who reminded Reb Nachman Kossover of the face of God. There are moments when we can catch that glow in the most ordinary of people, usually in moments of giving, caring, or somehow showing a generosity of spirit that opens their light to our view. At such a time, that person sheds ordinariness and becomes for us a momentary *tzaddik*. The light we see in that moment is that of Y-H-W-H, the One beyond all form. The same Being beyond names, or unspeakable Word beyond and within all words, is also the eternal source of inner light. As the One calls us into being, so does it cry out from within us to seek out its light in others, to brighten the light that glows within ourselves, and to draw others to that light. Our sharing of the light is the beginning of our homeward journey.

Hope and Transformation

Rabbi Nancy Wechsler-Azen

I n our society, a sense of shame often accompanies sadness and pain. We fear we burden others when our grief wells up like waves upon the sea. We worry that friends will abandon us if our pain has not abated. The fear of being "too much" for friends or family members keeps us stuck in loneliness. Ironically, it is often through our relationships with others that we feel connected with life.

When you are suffering, you need someone who will listen to your outpouring as many times as you need to say it. If you feel the need to do so, express your fear of being "too much." Don't let your unspoken words keep you suffering in solitude. You may choose to seek help from your rabbi. You may choose to seek out a counselor to help you walk through the jungle of despair. Through talking, the cloud of isolation often lifts and permits the very first breath of hope to enter....

One of the aspects of trauma that is often unacknowledged is that our soul goes through an extensive stretch as we progress through the crisis. We will never look at the world the same way because, in ways that no one will ever see, we are different: we have felt waves of grief, we have felt the healing of a good moment, we have learned to love ourselves and project love to others. We are transformed through consciousness. Some call this *teshuvah*, which means returning to God.

Once there was a fire in Breslov. Afterward Rabbi Nathan and a few others went to see where the fire had been. Rabbi Nathan saw the man whose house had burned down. The man had been crying terribly, looking to see if he could find any pieces of wood or metal he could salvage to use in rebuilding his house. He was collecting the pieces one by one. Rabbi Nathan said

Excerpted from *Surviving a Crisis or a Tragedy*, a LifeLight™ pastoral care pamphlet (Jewish Lights) by **Rabbi Nancy Wechsler-Azen**, the founding rabbi of Temple Kol Ami in Thornhill, Ontario, and current rabbi of Congregation Beth Shalom in Carmichael, California.

to his companions, "Did you see? Even though his house has burned down he hasn't given up hope of rebuilding it again. He is collecting everything he'll need when it comes to building. The same is true in spiritual life. The harshness of life battles with us to the point where we are almost completely burned up, but we must never give up hope. We must pick up a few good points within ourselves and collect them together from amid the troubles we have. This is what it means to return to God."

God Is Right Here and Right Now

Rabbi Joseph B. Meszler

A difficult but central belief for a Jewish theology of healing for today is a deep understanding of God being present in our lives. Many people might say that this is well and good for "believers," but what about the rest of us? Belief, however, does not have to be limited to faith in a Big Man Upstairs Who Controls Everything. God's presence instead can be thought of as an abiding, loving strength within people and all creation. In fact, the deepest things most of us believe in, such as truth, love, and compassion, are intangible but real parts of ourselves. Trying to live without confidence in a spiritual reality is like trying to live in a big black hole of despair. An unexpected touch of kindness from another can renew our faith that there is an inescapable power of goodness in the world.

This belief is rooted in the Hebrew Bible in the Book of Psalms. Many people turn to the Psalms for solace and for their acknowledgment of suffering, and much has been written about using the Psalms in prayer. The Psalms have also served as inspiration for all subsequent Jewish poetry. Perhaps the reason the Psalms speak to so many people is because in the Psalms God is understood to be present and available to people everywhere and at all times:

> How can I escape from Your spirit?
> How can I flee from Your face?
> If I go up to heaven, there You are;
> if I go down to the pit, You are here.

Excerpted from *Facing Illness, Finding God: How Judaism Can Help You and Caregivers Cope When Body or Spirit Fails* (Jewish Lights) by **Rabbi Joseph B. Meszler**, a noted spiritual leader and educator, and rabbi at Temple Sinai in Sharon, Massachusetts. His other books include *Witnesses to the One: The Spiritual History of the Sh'ma* (also Jewish Lights).

If I lift up on the wings of dawn,
lie down on the far edge of the sea,
also there Your hand will guide me,
Your right hand will grasp me tight.
If I say, "But darkness will hide me,
night will be my light,"
darkness is not too dark for You;
night is as bright as day;
as is the darkness, so is the light.

Psalm 139:7–12

It is precisely in the darkest moments that the psalmist asks us to turn to God who is everywhere: "Out of the depths I call to You, Eternal One! Sovereign, listen to my voice!" (Psalm 130:1–2). Even in a place where we feel completely abandoned and alone or whenever we try to run away and not face the challenges before us, our biblical ancestors had faith that God was there with us. The prophet Jeremiah echoed this theme when he declared, "'Am I a God who is only nearby,' says the Eternal, 'and not [also] God from far away? If someone hides in a hiding place, can I not see him?' says the Eternal. 'For do I not fill heaven and earth?'" (Jeremiah 23:23–24).

Solomon ibn Gabirol, a Hebrew poet from Spain, articulated the idea of God's omnipresence and the futility of running away from God with this memorable line: "I flee from You to You."[1] Even as we hustle from chore to chore, from office to home and home to office, from house to emergency room, we are not abandoned by God. God is everywhere. God is with the person who is sick in the room right here and now, and God is also with those who care for that person as they heed God's commandments by providing medical care, visiting, calling, or simply sending a note. God is with both the one in need of healing who suffers and the one who tries to heal. The God-like in us reaches out to the God-like in another. Dimensions of the Divine reach toward each other.

The Sages even took the idea of God's omnipresence another radical step, surpassing the idea of God being the soul of the universe. In their thinking, it is a mistake to think of God as a person or a power floating around the universe. For them, God is not only within the world, but God also transcends it. The universe does not contain God. Instead, God contains the universe.

The Rabbis articulated this belief in this way: "The Holy One of Blessing is the dwelling place of the world; it is not the world that is the dwelling place of God" (*Genesis Rabbah* 68:9). God is both near and far.[2] God is close by in the commandments we follow and in the prayers we say, and yet God is also incomprehensibly above and beyond our understanding. One prayer book puts it this way, "You are as close to us as breathing, yet You are farther than the farthermost star."[3]

If we believe that God can be found within and through people, if we believe that there is no place devoid of God's presence and love, and if we believe that there is no place where we may not pray and access the Divine, then we have to believe that God is present with us right here and right now. In every home, in every bedroom, in every building, and in every hospital room or hospice care facility, God is there. Even as you, the reader, hold this book, God is in the room with you right now.

Receiving Divine Light

Nan Fink Gefen, PhD

I n this meditation we focus on the light of the Divine. With each breath we receive it and experience its presence, using the same meditative technique found in other focused meditations.

You can relate to this meditation in a literal way or a metaphorical way. Some of you will have no difficulty envisioning God as light; others will be more comfortable thinking of light as creative or healing energy, holy in its own way.

Through the centuries Jewish mystics devised many meditations on divine light. They saw light as a manifestation of God, and especially liked to contemplate its different qualities. At times they stared at burning candles or performed various eye movements to see the spectrum of its colors.

The divine light meditation is a contemporary meditation, but it parallels many found in the Jewish mystical tradition. It is often used with beginning students because it helps them have an immediate spiritual connection with the Divine. We teach that God as divine light infuses the universe and is available to everyone. Like the air we breathe, it is everywhere—even in a darkened room—but we are usually unaware of its presence.

The imagery of divine light is found throughout Judaism. In the Torah we read that God's first act, after creating heaven and earth, was to create light: "And God said, 'Let there be light.' And there was light" (Genesis 1:3).

The understanding of God as creator of light is present also within the liturgy. In one of the blessings before the *Shema* in the morning service, we praise God for bringing on the morning light after the dark of night, and we end with, "Blessed is *Adonai*, Creator of light(s)."

Excerpted from *Discovering Jewish Meditation*, 2nd Edition: *Instruction and Guidance for Learning an Ancient Spiritual Practice* (Jewish Lights) by **Nan Fink Gefen, PhD**, cofounder of *Tikkun* magazine and the meditation center Chochmat HaLev in Berkeley, California.

The connection between God and light goes even further. Not only does God *create* light, but God *is* light. Light radiates outward, through the universe, in a multitude of hues. Toward the end of the *Amidah* in the prayer book, we find the phrase, "Bless us, our God, with the light of Your presence."

Isaac Luria, the sixteenth-century Kabbalist, spoke about the beginning of existence when the entire universe was God as divine essence. God then contracted to make room for creation to take place. Divine light emanated through the space that was opened, and it is still present today for all of us to receive. The *kavannah* (intention) of the divine light meditation is to open yourself to the light of the Divine.

Practice: Divine Light Meditation

Once you have settled on your cushion or chair, take several slow, deep breaths. Make a sound with each exhalation, letting go of the pressures of the day.

Now begin to breathe regularly.

Breath in.
Breath out.

With each inhalation, receive the light of the Divine.
Experience its beauty and boundless strength.
Its color
Its warmth
Its radiance
Its cascading creative energy.

With each breath in, the light of the Divine fills you.
It gives you a feeling of well-being
Clarity
Strength.

With each exhalation, the light of the Divine passes through you.
Healing you
Cleansing you
Releasing the toxins of your everyday life.

With each in-breath, receiving the presence of divine light.

With each out-breath, experiencing the gift of divine light.

When your thoughts wander, as they inevitably will, gently encircle them with light and return to the focus of the meditation.

Breath in.

Breath out.

If you become distracted by a sound or a movement around you, notice it, then return to the focus of the meditation.

Divine light.

God's presence.

Choose Life

Rabbi Rachel Cowan

One cold winter's afternoon I was walking in a park in New York City. The air was absolutely clear. A sharp cold breeze sliced through my jacket. Huddling for warmth, I looked around me. Suddenly everything appeared to be frozen in space and time. The walls, the walkways, the river, the trees seemed like empty shapes. The world, I perceived, has no content, only form. It is cold and empty. That perception was excruciating. Then a phrase from the Torah—from the Book of Deuteronomy—rose in my mind. God, speaking through Moses to the people of Israel, said, "I have put before you life and death ... choose life!" I felt as if Moses were speaking to me. I also felt myself in the company of others who have suffered painful loss throughout thousands of years. If they had made it through these hard times, so could I.

Choosing life means committing to life, committing to its fullness, hanging on through the downs, and enjoying the ups. It means accepting death as a part of life. I looked up and saw other people walking in the park. I was not alone. I knew my future lay in relationships with them, not in cultivating the solitary bleakness in my heart.

The Book of Psalms is a treasury for those of us who seek spiritual comfort. These 150 poems convey in exquisite beauty the full range of human emotions, from abject despair to complete joy. I found several psalms that reflected different phases of my healing journey, and I would read them often. The poetry expressed many of my emotions and introduced me to ancient spiritual companions. My four favorite psalms that reflect the journey from the depths of pain to the comfort of faith are Psalms 88, 42, 30, and 23.

When I am feeling the pain of loss and loneliness, these lines from Psalm 88 speak for me:

Excerpted from *Coping with the Death of a Spouse*, a LifeLight™ pastoral care pamphlet (Jewish Lights) by **Rabbi Rachel Cowan**, senior fellow and cofounder of the Institute for Jewish Spirituality.

> O Lord, God of my deliverance,
> when I cry out in the night before You,
> let my prayer reach You;
> incline Your ear to my cry.
> For I am sated with misfortune....
> Why O Lord, do You reject me,
> do You hide Your face from me?

When I am wondering why my loved one died and how I will stand up straight again, I find affirmation of my questions in these lines from Psalm 42:

> Why so downcast, my soul,
> why disquieted within me?
> Have hope in God;
> I will yet praise Him
> for His saving presence.

And then, when I am feeling strong and joyful, I recall these lines from Psalm 30:

> O Lord, my God,
> I cried out to You,
> and You healed me....
> O you faithful of the Lord, sing to Him
> and praise His holy name.
> For He is angry but a moment,
> and when He is pleased there is life.
> One may lie down weeping at nightfall,
> but at dawn there are shouts of joy.

Often when I am going to sleep, feeling the need for support and security, I think of Psalm 23:

> The Lord is my shepherd, I shall not want.
> He maketh me to lie down in green pastures;
> He leadeth me beside the still waters. He restoreth my soul....
> Yea though I walk through the valley of the shadow of death,
> I will fear no evil, for Thou art with me;
> Thy rod and Thy staff, they comfort me....

Gradually I came to understand that fairness is not the ruling principle in the universe. Some good people die too early, and some bad people live too long. Why my loved one died is an irrelevant question. Nobody can answer it, and even if they could, what answer would be acceptable? The question is: Now that this horrible thing has happened, how do I continue to hope, express compassion, and appreciate the beauty of life? How do I open myself to God's presence?

May God Remember

Rabbi Lawrence A. Hoffman, PhD

What possible sense can it make to say that God remembers? Can God, then, also forget? Is that why we remind God to remember us? Put another way, isn't memory a temporal function, and thus beyond God who is eternal? ...

The Rabbis treated God's memory other than we do; it was, for them, a spatial, not a temporal thing.... We can variously live in the present, the future, or the past, as our mental health requires. It makes sense for humans to think in terms of time.

But what about God, who, we say, is *melekh ha'olam*, "ruler of the world"? If an earthly monarch, "a king of flesh and blood" (*melekh basar vadam*), as the Rabbis put it, were to rule the whole earth, would he also be *melekh ha'olam*, do you suppose? The answer is no, because such a ruler would hold sway only over the *space* of the earth, but not its existence in *time*. God, by contrast, is *melekh ha'olam*, but also, *mei'atah v'ad olam*, "from now until eternity"—when applied to God, *olam* has the sense of space *and* time, for God lives in time the way humans live in space. That is the Rabbis' best philosophical insight—the insistence that time is to God what space is to us.

God, then, does not "remember" the way we do. To remind God of something is not just to dredge up some old memory that was once alive but now is only a faded outline of what it was when it was "real." Reminding God about an instance in time is more akin to pointing out to humans a distant place on the map of space, which thereby moves into focus, if you like, even though it never actually stopped being there. The closest *we humans* can come is the science fiction of time travel, when we imagine that time is space and

Excerpted from *May God Remember: Memory and Memorializing in Judaism—Yizkor* in the *Prayers of* Awe series (Jewish Lights), edited by **Rabbi Lawrence A. Hoffman, PhD**, author of over thirty books, world-renowned liturgist, and holder of the Stephen and Barbara Friedman Chair in Liturgy, Worship and Ritual at Hebrew Union College–Jewish Institute of Religion in New York.

that, like the *Star Trek* team, we can awaken one morning to find ourselves not just with memories but with the reality of Al Capone's Chicago or Julius Caesar's Rome. Travelers in time or space need pointers to show the way. And that is where *zekher/zikaron* [both words meaning "memory" or "memorial" or sometimes even "reminder"] comes into play for God. *Zekher/zikaron* is not a memorial; it is a pointer.... With regard to our deceased, it is as if we understand that they are dead only from the perspective of human beings, for whom space is unending but time is not. In God's mind's eye, however, time too is all-present, so that even those who die are as alive as ever. We point them out to God.

On the High Holy Days, we are asked to stretch our mind to the point of imagining that we see things as God does. Rosh Hashanah and Yom Kippur provide this sweeping vision of a universe of space and time that is visible, in its entirety and all at once—but only to the eternal perspective of God. The map, however, is neither homogeneous nor static; it has shifting highlights, and the highlighted areas are open to our design. We can weigh the relative significance of different points on the map, "reminding" God to attend to this quadrant rather than that. One of the grandest things we aspire to do is point God's way to our beloved who have passed from that quadrant of time that houses us but who still remain alive in the eternity of time that God alone inhabits.

This foray into liturgical theology says something also about the character of human beings. In this religious anthropology, we are not mere victims of the grains of sand that descend inexorably in the hourglass of being and bury us under a virtual *tel* of time, as if we had never existed; nor, in our own lives, need we feel inundated by the detritus of civilization gone awry, the screaming headlines and mega-events that relegate us to mere statistics in a universe that is presumed to be too impersonal and too large to keep us in mind.

The grand message of God's memory is that human beings are never out of mind. They may always be kept in mind, because our liturgy evokes their existence in the mind of God. Liturgy is the means by which they are pointed out, visited, remembered, even saved. There can be no nobler hallmark of the human spirit than this: the chutzpah to believe that even the lowliest human being is worthy of God's attention and that human culture at its best calls us together, even across generations, to be remembered by God, pointed out on the divine map of eternity!

Troubles

Rebbe Nachman of Breslov

Kind, loving, mighty God:
Stretch out Your hand
to strengthen me.
Lift me up
from my abyss;
right my wrongs;
turn my every failure
into success.
Look upon all my troubles
and say,
"Enough!"

Likutei Moharan 1:195

Excerpted from *The Gentle Weapon: Prayers for Everyday and Not-So-Everyday Moments—Timeless Wisdom from the Teachings of the Hasidic Master, Rebbe Nachman of Breslov* (Jewish Lights), adapted by Moshe Mykoff and S. C. Mizrahi, together with the Breslov Research Institute. **Rebbe Nachman of Breslov** (1772–1810), founder of Breslov Hasidism, is best known for his stories and teachings on mitzvah and relationship with God.

Living with Uncertainty

Dr. David Hartman

The amazing message of the biblical story of the manna is that God enters into a relationship with a people who cannot live with uncertainty. The story would have been nice and uplifting if Israel had gathered just enough manna for one day and said, "God, we trust you." Instead, the story relates that Israel gathered more than enough manna for one day, hoarding away extra, which invariably rotted. God, as it were, had asked them: "Can you not spend one night sleeping with uncertainty?" But they responded: "No. We do not have the strength to trust!"...

Israel in its limitations is accepted by God, as is Israel who builds a golden calf and Israel who wants to return to Egypt every time water or food is in short supply. Israel in sin and rebellion is still loved because God's covenant is based on what human beings really are. If it were based on unrealistic divine expectations, I would be frightened of accepting the Sinai covenant. But because of the frank descriptions of Israel's failures, I know that the divine demand (mitzvah) is grounded in reality. The divine commandments (*mitzvot*) are given to vulnerable, fragile human beings. When I put on *tefillin* (phylacteries) and pray in the morning, it is not human grandeur that is being acknowledged but rather human vulnerability and imperfection. I can love God and sense God's acceptance of me as a weak, finite human being. I am a "commanded one" within the context of human limitations.

The covenant thus signifies the restored dignity of the concrete and the finite. It expresses the ability to love in spite of human limitations, to build meaning in the face of death, to act today without certainty about tomorrow. George Steiner is mistaken when he claims that "tragedy is alien to the Judaic sense of the world." One has only to read the Book of Job to realize that Job's

Excerpted from *A Heart of Many Rooms: Celebrating the Many Voices within Judaism* (Jewish Lights) by **Dr. David Hartman**, world-renowned philosopher and social activist, founder and president emeritus of the Shalom Hartman Institute in Jerusalem, and author of many award-winning books.

problem was never resolved. God does not answer Job's questions at the end of the story, but, as Maimonides understood, Job gained a new perception of history and God. People may think the Book of Job has a happy ending, but anyone who has experienced the death of a child knows how painful it is to love after undergoing such a tragic loss. Yet Job had the courage to start a new family in spite of the tragic uncertainty of life.

Death invades our lives, often making our dreams and aspirations into a joke. Yet, knowing that we are frail and vulnerable, we still love and build families. We know our weaknesses, yet we take our lives very seriously. Can we live with that kind of tension? For many people, this is impossible unless they can believe in a total and final resolution to human suffering through eternity, through redemption, through the ultimate liberation from death....

Can you live with uncertainty, or must you have absolute, ironclad truths whereby God discloses to you: "This is My way; follow it and you are saved; deviate from it and you are lost"? Do we need absolute certainty in order to build a spiritual way of life?

Singing in Despair

Rabbi Maurice Lamm

¹ Give thanks to Adonai, call upon His name;
  Let all nations know about His deeds!
² Sing to Him, compose songs, play instruments for Him;
  Tell all about His wondrous acts!
³ Take pride in His Holy Name;
  The heart of those who seek Him rejoices!
⁴ Search for Adonai and for His might,
  Seek His presence always!
⁵ Remember the wonders He has performed,
  His miracles, and the laws from His mouth....
²⁸ He sent darkness—and it was dark;
  they did not rebel against His word....
³⁹ He spread out a cloud as a sheltering cover,
  a fire to illumine the night.
⁴⁰ Israel asked and He provided quail,
  He satisfied them with bread from Heaven.
⁴¹ He broke open a rock and waters gushed out,
  rushing through dry places like a river.
⁴² For He remembered His holy word, His promise
  to Abraham, His servant.
⁴³ He brought out His people with gladness,
  His chosen ones with joyful singing.
⁴⁴ He gave them the lands of nations,
  they inherited that which nations acquire by labor.

Excerpted from *Healing of Soul, Healing of Body: Spiritual Leaders Unfold the Strength and Solace in Psalms* (Jewish Lights), edited by Rabbi Simkha Y. Weintraub, CSW. **Rabbi Maurice Lamm** is president of the National Institute for Jewish Hospice and former rabbi of Beth Jacob Congregation in Beverly Hills, California.

[45] So that they might keep His statutes,
and treasure His teachings,
Halleluyah![1]

Psalm 105

What's the value of a song? In our sophistication, we think of singing as an art form; but the Torah teaches that to sing is a blessing. In terms of the spirit, singing is on a higher level than speaking—it is why the Levites sang in the Temple. The word *shir*, meaning song, also derives from *shur*, meaning insight. When we sing we raise our souls to God, and we gain insight into Him. Through song we address God.

And through song we learn to better endure our hardships. When life is not a song, sing! When King David was ill, he sang; when Cervantes, the great writer, was ill, he said: "He who sings frightens away his ills." Ask yourself: Why do people always smile when they sing? Singing is an antidote to panic. The Hasidim taught us that. It lightens the burden, lessens the fear, steadies the nerves. Singing gives voice to our deepest feelings; it enables us to express ourselves even if we are the only ones who hear it. And we will have made ourselves heard. Singing lifts the heart.

Even if all we do is chant "Oy Vay," over and over, to a tune we improvise— *Shiru lo*, "Sing to Him." Even a melancholy song somehow takes us out of ourselves and gives expression to our inner being. Sometimes I break out in a *niggun*—a melody that uses sounds shaped only by my emotions. It articulates a groan that forces its way out of my interior; sometimes it expresses an indescribable joy inside me that's in search of an audience.

Sometimes we sing a familiar *niggun* with friends with whom we sway in oneness. It crystallizes our common despair, and the sadness gets dissipated in fellowship. It harmonizes our own souls with the souls of those who empathize with us. The harmony, in magical ways, transfers the energy of the group to us fragile individuals as we lift up our voices and keep time together.

Sing what you like; help others by offering to sing with them. Especially effective may be a mother's *niggun*, one that she sang for us at bedtime or when we were sick. We can sing from religious songs; old nursery rhymes; oldies but goodies; college songs—if they make us smile or help us to express our anxiety. If you feel the onset of despair, sing out your despair in a *niggun*.

To groan when we are in pain is common; to sing is courageous.

Restoring
Your Soul

God restores my soul....
Surely goodness and mercy will follow me
all the days of my life.

Psalm 23:3, 6

Y ou have been changed forever by your loss. As you seek to reorient your-self to the new world around you, let the blessings of your loved one's legacy live on in you. Seek out the goodness and mercy in the world, and help those around you see it, too. Do your best to make active choices about how you want to live, who you want to be, and how to let the Divine Light shine through the cracks in your heart.

It takes a long time to feel like your soul has been restored. Yet even in the midst of grieving, some days you catch a glimpse, out of the corner of your eye, of goodness and mercy following you.

Facing a Cascade of Losses

Rabbi Dayle A. Friedman, MSW, MA, BCC

The Book of Ruth opens with Naomi, a woman who has endured unimaginable suffering. Naomi, formerly a denizen of Bethlehem, in the Land of Israel, was forced by famine to decamp to Moab, along with her husband, Elimelech, and two sons, Machlon and Chilion. While in Moab, her sons took local women, Ruth and Orpah, as wives. As the biblical narrative opens, Naomi is returning home to Bethlehem after the untimely deaths of her husband and two sons. She has instructed her daughters-in-law to return to their families, but one, Ruth, insists on accompanying her.

Without her husband and sons, Naomi is shorn of nearly everything she once treasured—love, income, stability, and social station. Once again uprooted, she returns to her former home, but she is not the same. When the local women spy her approaching, they say, "Can this be Naomi?" She replies, "Do not call me Naomi [pleasantness]. Call me Mara [bitterness], for the Almighty has made my lot very bitter. I went away full, and God has brought me back empty. How can you call me Naomi, when God has dealt harshly with me, when the Almighty has brought misfortune upon me!" (Ruth 1:19–21). This once proud woman has utterly succumbed to despair.

Amazingly, Naomi starts over. She ingeniously engineers a marriage for Ruth, thereby protecting her from the physical and economic vulnerability of being a woman on her own. Naomi identifies Boaz, a distant relative with a legal obligation to marry a childless widow of a family member. She instructs Ruth to place herself at the feet of the sleeping Boaz, thereby putting him in a compromising position so that he will feel compelled to fulfill his duty. The scheme works. Boaz marries Ruth and they have a child, Obed, grandfather

Excerpted from *Jewish Wisdom for Growing Older: Finding Your Grit and Grace Beyond Midlife* (Jewish Lights) by **Rabbi Dayle A. Friedman, MSW, MA, BCC**, who offers training, consulting, and spiritual guidance through Growing Older, her Philadelphia-based national practice. Rabbi Friedman is also editor of *Jewish Pastoral Care: A Practical Handbook from Traditional and Contemporary Sources* (also Jewish Lights).

of King David, and progenitor of the messianic line. Thus Naomi has ensured a promising future, not just for Ruth but for the entire world.

At the end of the story, the townswomen once again address Naomi. They say, "Blessed be the Eternal, who has not withheld a redeemer from you today! May his name be perpetuated in Israel! He will renew your life and sustain your old age; for he is born of your daughter-in-law, who loves you and is better to you than seven sons." Naomi becomes the nursemaid for the baby, and the women declare, "A son is born to Naomi!" (Ruth 4:14–17).

What Keeps Us Going in the Face of Losses?

Naomi has somehow weathered an immense accumulation of losses. She has begun again. She has built a new life and a future. How has she found the strength, courage, and determination to move forward after all she has been through? What can we learn from her about the sources of resiliency for us as we face loss?

Allowing Grief

Naomi certainly does not whitewash the pain of her situation. She gives her sadness vivid expression when she demands to be called *Mara*—bitterness. She names her losses, saying, "I went away full, and God has brought me back empty" (Ruth 1:20). We can easily imagine that Naomi has screamed and wailed plenty. Feeling her pain and giving it expression are very possibly important aspects of her capacity to move forward amid it.

Sandy is a ninety-year-old scientist. Although she is officially retired, she is still involved in publishing her groundbreaking research. Her husband died years ago, as did her daughter. Last year Sandy's beloved granddaughter died suddenly at the age of twenty-six, shortly after Sandy moved from her longtime home to live with her children. Sandy reports, "I wrestle all night. I cry, I ask *why* I had to lose all of them. But when I wake up in the morning, I discover I am excited about the day that lies ahead." Perhaps Sandy's fearlessness in facing the raw pain of her losses creates the space to also find joy in the life she has.

Naomi and Sandy do not resist or deny their grief. They do not pretend that they are undiminished or unscathed. Rather, they give voice to their sorrow, either in conversation or in the quiet of their beds in the darkest moments of night. They are also profoundly engaged with others.

Love

Love is a powerful engine of resiliency. Naomi's love for Ruth provides her with a reason to start over. She simply cannot let her daughter-in-law, who has so lovingly and loyally stuck by her side, die of hunger or be utterly vulnerable to abuse. Naomi manages to thrive amid loss because she has someone to love and someone to care for and because she dedicates herself, through her grandson, to the betterment of the future.

Of course, having friends or family to offer us love when we are bereft is healing. But Naomi teaches us that it is not just receiving love that salves our wounds. *Giving* our own love and caring can be salvific. When our attention is directed toward meeting another's needs, we often find that our own sorrows recede into the background.... Our losses can open us up to deep empathy and make us uniquely available to others. Remarkably, as we discover how much love we have, we are empowered to go on.

Savoring Gifts

It might seem paradoxical but along with acknowledging and feeling our losses, finding gratitude for what we *have* can help us reclaim our wholeness. Often as we and our lives are changed by what is no longer here, new blessings crop up—new or deeper relationships with people who show up for us, heightened awareness of beauty, or perhaps a new sense of our own strength. For Naomi, the birth of a grandson was a remarkable and hopeful delight....

Jewish tradition teaches us to say blessings, to express appreciation, for all kinds of experiences, positive and negative. As you ponder loss, take time as well to cultivate gratitude. For centuries, the traditional prayer for waking up in the morning known as *Modeh/Modah Ani* (I give thanks) was the first taught to young children. This prayer calls us to cherish the very fact of our continued existence. Whatever threats or dangers you have encountered, you are still here. You get to embrace another day.

A Blessing

As you face loss, may you open your heart wide.
May you feel sorrow in all its depths and still embrace tiny joys.
May you take in kindness and savor what you have and have had.

How Can We Go On?

Rabbi Bradley Shavit Artson, DHL

We live in a world that is often chaotic, in which our most sublime hopes are made ridiculous and our most cherished connections are inevitably sundered. We live under the shadow of that reality—the awareness of what the world is like—even when times are good.

The central challenge confronting all of us, all humanity, is how to live in the face of incoherence and chaos. What is good? What does God require of us? How can we fashion meaning and community when our lives are in the grip of absurdity and happenstance?

The world has no shame. At funerals, I've often felt embarrassed as we bury the remains of a lovely and caring human being while the sun still shines, the birds still fly, and the voices of children at play waft from beyond the confines of the cemetery. As a rabbi, I have literally driven from a baby-naming celebration to a funeral to a wedding.

How dare the world go on? How can we stand to dance, knowing that in the midst of our community, friends and family are wrestling with unspeakable loss or limitless fear?

Yet we do go on, and life does continue. We are held in the indifferent pincers of time and human nature, unable to wriggle free. "It was not your will that formed you, nor was it your will that gave you birth; it is not your will that makes you live, and it is not your will that brings you death" (*Pirkei Avot* 4:29). We are trapped on a roller coaster that will not stop and will not shift its course.

Excerpted from *Passing Life's Tests: Spiritual Reflections on the Trial of Abraham, the Binding of Isaac* (Jewish Lights) by **Rabbi Bradley Shavit Artson, DHL**, who holds the Abner and Roslyn Goldstine Dean's Chair of the Ziegler School of Rabbinic Studies and is vice president of American Jewish University in Los Angeles. Rabbi Artson's other books include *God of Becoming and Relationship: The Dynamic Nature of Process Theology* (also Jewish Lights).

Knowing all that, how can we go on living? How can we make meaning and shelter for each other and ourselves in the world as it really is?

For the spiritual person, the central arena in the struggle of life is not just the world. Society can change slowly, and individuals gradually acquire new insight. But the pain and senselessness of aging, illness, and death are eternal. All humanity is locked into the vise of time. As it moves, we age, advance, let go. The world does not change; we do.

Which means, as I indicated already, that the primary arena of response to the reality of the world is in the human heart, the human soul. How we respond to the world can spell the difference between hope and meaning on the one hand, and despair and irrelevance on the other. How *we* respond....

Elie Wiesel, upon receiving the Nobel Prize in 1986, remarked in his acceptance speech, "We know that every moment is a moment of grace, every hour an offering." His words echo the gratitude of our ancient prayer to God: "In Your goodness, day after day You renew creation."

How do we balance the piercing intensity of the present with the persistent call of the future? By returning to the earliest mission of our ancient ways, by returning to God. For, ultimately, eternity and the present meet in the loving heart of God. The Holy Ancient One who always was and will always be, the Fount of life and hope of humanity, is the One for whom present, past, and future coexist. By making ourselves known to God, by cultivating gratitude and holiness that can pervade every aspect of our lives—how we work, how we live, and how we play—we fuse the eternal and the instant.

Crying and Sighing

Rebbe Nachman of Breslov

The years have brought
more pain
than ever I imagined possible.
When I cry,
loving God,
let me cry only to You.
When I sigh,
let that sigh
be a pure, honest expression
of a soul yearning
for Your Light.
Let my cries and sighs
heal me
and restore me
and bring me to joy.
Let me never again succumb
to bitterness
or depressing thoughts.
God,
show me life's meaning.

Likutei Moharan 1:56

Excerpted from *The Gentle Weapon: Prayers for Everyday and Not-So-Everyday Moments—Timeless Wisdom from the Teachings of the Hasidic Master, Rebbe Nachman of Breslov* (Jewish Lights), adapted by Moshe Mykoff and S. C. Mizrahi, together with the Breslov Research Institute. **Rebbe Nachman of Breslov** (1772–1810), founder of Breslov Hasidism, is best known for his stories and teachings on mitzvah and relationship with God.

How to Become a Blessing

Rabbi Elie Kaplan Spitz
with Erica Shapiro Taylor

In studying the Torah's descriptions of God's despair and healing, we find insights for our own lives. God shows us how to respond to despair: articulating pain, pausing before acting, hearing a message of hope, crafting an identity of mercy and compassion, choosing to see the world as good, and going on to become a blessing. God in our tradition models heroic healing.

These descriptions of God are surprising, because most of us were taught that God is all-knowing and perfect. Yet here is a God that longs for relationship, as defined by the covenant, only to experience pain and choose reconciliation. In my counseling, I often ask those dealing with despair to write a letter to God, to write as if God were the recipient. The letters are composed with honesty, because we expect that God knows us and our secrets. This conversation elicits clarity and catharsis, which is the nature of heartfelt prayer. I then ask the writers to respond to their letters as if they were God. Responding from God's vantage point signifies divine empathy. I find that the responses "from God" offer direction, love, and acceptance.

Our process of healing ourselves and others begins with acknowledging that we are shattered vessels that contain divine sparks. To become a blessing, to offer compassion and hope and healing, we must begin with humility. The word "blessing" in Hebrew, *brachah*, has a three-letter root that also appears in the word *birkayim* for knees and *breichah*, meaning a pool of water.[1] To be a blessing is to come before God in humility, upon our knees, aware of our own vulnerability and our own flaws. To be a blessing is to accept with gratitude

Excerpted from *Healing from Despair: Choosing Wholeness in a Broken World* (Jewish Lights) by Rabbi Elie Kaplan Spitz with Erica Shapiro Taylor. **Rabbi Elie Kaplan Spitz** is a spiritual leader and scholar specializing in topics of spirituality and Judaism, and rabbi of Congregation B'nai Israel in Tustin, California. His other books include *Does the Soul Survive? A Jewish Journey to Belief in Afterlife, Past Lives and Living with Purpose* (also Jewish Lights).

that creation, as represented by a pool of water, is beyond our comprehension and contains an abundance of goodness. A blessing is a humble prayer to God asking God to bestow the abundance of life upon our loved ones.

To see the world through God's eyes in the biblical tradition is to acknowledge that the world is at once broken and good. God saw the good in creation on six successive days and saw the corruption of that creation on repeated occasions. Each time God encountered betrayal, God despaired, paused to see the world with grace and hope, then forgave. As God heeded the message of hope from Abraham, Noah, and Moses, so we must remain open to a message of healing. As God forgave the people after the episode of the golden calf for their infidelity, so we are called to forgive those who have hurt us. As God on seeing Noah accepted humanity despite corruption, so we must accept that brokenness exists alongside profound kindness. As God chose not to act from blind anger on hearing the report of the emissaries, but recognized the fears and limitations of the people, so we must move past anger toward understanding and healing. Forgiveness is not the denial of a wrong done, but an understanding and acceptance of the source of the wrong and the willingness to reclaim relationship. Forgiving ourselves means recognizing our capacity for the work of repair. To forgive is to unload weights that burden us and to proclaim that we who are created in God's image can become a blessing.

We are called upon to be a blessing. To be a blessing is God's promise to Abraham, to the people at Mount Sinai, and beyond. To be a blessing is a challenge and a duty, for all peoples. We are to look to God as the source of our inner, sacred sparks and we are to collect those sparks by imitating God's goodness. In Deuteronomy 11:22, God instructs the people to follow all of the commandments, walking in God's ways and cleaving to God. The Rabbis comment as follows on the call to walk in God's ways: "These are the ways of the Holy One.... [T]his means that just as God is gracious and compassionate, you too must be gracious and compassionate."[2]

Losses impose heavy burdens upon us. Under the weight of the burdens we may find ourselves in a deep, dark, lonely place.... Amid the shattered bits of our broken selves, we can uncover divine sparks, and with them bring light to others. Even in the grip of suffering we can choose: choose to listen to the message of hope, choose to craft our identity, choose to accept a worldview of faith in the good in the world, and choose to discover our calling in healing the world. As Moses told the people, we are reminded: "You shall not corrupt the judgment of a proselyte or orphan, you shall not take the garment of a widow as a pledge. You shall remember that you were a slave in Egypt, and the Ever-Present-One, your God, redeemed you from there, therefore I command you to do this thing" (Deuteronomy 24:17). We can choose to make the experience of pain a crucible of compassion for the needy and of humility in serving the most vulnerable.

As shattered vessels we hold fast to shards that can reflect the light of a good world into the dark corners of souls in despair. Our experiences in a place of darkness leave us forever changed, mindful of the comfort a listener can bring. Our time spent suffering teaches us that a thoughtful listener can lighten the burdens that overwhelm us. Our own moments of pain show us that a caring listener is a blessing. Through our own despair we may become a source of comfort and hope to others. In the words of *The Big Book of Alcoholics Anonymous*, this simple but paradoxical truth is expressed as follows:

> Showing others who suffer how we were given help is the very thing which makes life seem so worthwhile to us now. Cling to the thought that, in God's hands, the dark past is the greatest possession you have—the key to life and happiness for others. With it you can avert death and misery for them.[3]

Although the world in which we live is broken, we have every reason to say, "It is good." And more, to do good, to live a life that is more whole and responds to God's call to live a life that is holy.... We are called to imitate God, to return again and again from hopelessness to hope, to see the world in all its brokenness filled with divine sparks. We are called to be a blessing: to alleviate suffering and to craft relationships grounded in love. And when we undertake the work of healing the world, we can look back on despair and look out on creation and echo God's words, "It is good."...

> *Rebono shel ha'olam*, source of mystery and presence,
> in this broken and beautiful world grant us the wisdom and
>   strength
> to draw on our despair to do Your work,
> the work of repairing brokenness,

collecting divine sparks,
and healing the pain of souls,
bit by bit.
May we echo Your words,
imitate Your deeds,
and serve as a blessing on Your behalf.
Amen.

Why Didn't You Enjoy All the Permitted Pleasures?

Rabbi Dannel I. Schwartz
with Mark Hass

H appiness wasn't something that just happened to Molly. Most of the people who know her would say just the opposite: That her past seven years had been filled with the kind of tragedy that would cripple the best of us and drive the rest close to mental or physical collapse.

Molly's twenty-four-year-old daughter died of a previously undiscovered congenital heart problem just two years before her husband was diagnosed with a deadly form of cancer. There was never even time to grieve properly, to relieve herself gradually of the burden of her child's death, to make herself whole. Her transition from mother of a dying child to wife of a dying man was nearly seamless.

Her husband died after three years of painful illness. Even though Molly knew his death was coming, even though they had talked about her life without him and how it would be when he passed from her, she was not prepared. The medical bills had exhausted their savings, the emotional roller coaster had sapped her strength. She felt immobilized, lost.

But only for a while.

I saw Molly fourteen months after her husband's death. She was on an outing at a professional baseball game with some coworkers. Molly had found a job to make ends meet. She had rediscovered something else: joy. She was interacting with everyone around her enthusiastically, as if she had not been touched by pain. She was having fun, and that's why she'd organized this visit

Excerpted from *Finding Joy: A Practical Spiritual Guide to Happiness* (Jewish Lights) by Rabbi Dannel I. Schwartz with Mark Hass. **Rabbi Dannel I. Schwartz** is founder and spiritual leader of Temple Shir Shalom in West Bloomfield, Michigan, and CEO of The Corners: A Campus for Caring Communities.

to the ballpark, even though she wasn't much of a baseball fan. Doing it gave her purpose: to make herself happy and make others happy in the process.

As I got to know this new Molly in the following months, I would realize that was the key to her happiness. By working at being happy, she had emerged from what could have been a life of anger, powerlessness, and sadness. Sure, she'd taken classes on how to cope with grief, read the usual books, listened to the advice of family and friends, and probably learned something from all of that. But her personal commitment to finding happiness and her willingness to work at it gave her a structure for pursuing a joyful life.

"I started by practicing the little things," she said. "If being alone was getting me down, I realized that I had to be with other people. But being with other people was difficult. So I practiced. I would get dressed up every morning, even though I had no place to go. By the time I realized the emptiness that surrounded me, the sympathy calls had stopped and people rarely called. So I called old friends. But they had husbands; they didn't have my hurt. So I chose people I knew would understand if I cried every now and then, or if I fell quiet during a conversation. These people were in similar situations to mine or were people I'd known a long time.

"It was difficult when I started, but that's what practicing is all about. At first, I practiced going to the movies with people. Before the movie, I talked about what we were going to see. After the movie, I talked about what we'd seen. After mastering that, I started practicing going to dinner with people, and then I practiced *really* talking with them. Then I got into a groove and out of my rut. Now, a day doesn't go by that I don't practice some aspect of living."

Those who say that Molly had repressed her true feelings would be wrong. In fact, Molly's approach is clearheaded and spiritual. It is consistent with teachings in the fundamental texts of Jewish mysticism, which hold remarkable insights for Jews and non-Jews alike who are searching for a happiness that seems to elude them.

The texts of the Kabbalah, the *Zohar,* the *Bahir*, and the *Sefer Yetzira,* in addition to mystical portions of the more familiar and accessible Talmud, have rarely been used to shape a practical conceptual basis for making life happier. That's a shame, because the mystics have some good advice about happiness. The Jewish mystical tradition is centered on the belief that with a spiritual focus, joy is possible and greater appreciation of the world is achievable, no matter what our problems or pain may be.

Practice: Exercises for the Soul

Monday   Look for opportunities to say "Thank you." Each time you say it, you will make two people happy. One of the major concepts of prayer is the expression of gratitude. When you say "Thank you," even to God, you show that you recognize and appreciate the gift that you've been given.

Tuesday   Be alone for twenty minutes near the end of the day. No television, no radio, no books, no newspapers. Commuting to and from work doesn't count. Just sit alone in a quiet place and think of the good things from your day. Reflect. Don't plan ahead. Savor the moment.

Wednesday   Buy or pick a single flower. Choose the most beautiful or the most fragrant. Take the flower home. Note its uniqueness. Treasure the reason you selected it. Now appreciate one aspect of yourself or of someone close to you that is special, unique, and beautiful.

Thursday   Apologize to someone you love. Do it the hard way. If it feels uncomfortable to write a letter, write one. If a personal apology would cause you the most distress, that's what you do. An apology is an act of clarity. It focuses us on the relationship between our actions and the feelings of others.

Friday   Treat yourself to a food you truly enjoy. Recite a blessing (any blessing that you choose) over it, before or after eating.

Saturday   Say something praiseworthy to someone. Say it so not only that person can hear it, but so others can as well.

Sunday   Do something special by yourself that you wouldn't normally do, but that you enjoy. Go see a specific painting at the museum or a certain animal you are curious about at the zoo or attend a concert at the symphony hall.

Who Will Lead the Seder, Now That I Stand Alone?

Rachel Josefowitz Siegel

How can I put loneliness into words? How can I convey what it's like to live alone after forty-six years of married life? How can I share what it is like to live Jewishly as a woman alone in her early seventies?

I cannot possibly enumerate the seemingly insignificant moments of daily life that I can no longer share: The things that my husband and I used to do together that I now do by myself, the things we always talked about that I now keep to myself, and the significant events that I now attend alone. At times, being alone is like a dull ache. At other times, it gives me a feeling of contentment and self-sufficiency. In some ways, I feel as if I have uncovered an inner strength that I did not fully know before. I am a little wiser, have overcome many fears and challenges, and have acquired new skills. I have made a few changes in my home that express more fully who I am, as well as doing justice to who we were together and as a family.

Some of the most profound adjustments to widowhood have been in the area of Jewish observance. When our children grew up and left home, I gradually accommodated to setting the Shabbat table for two instead of five, and celebrating the High Holy Days as a couple instead of a family. But that was nothing compared to coming to terms with eating alone on Friday night or going to *shul* by myself.

When my husband, Ben, died five years ago, I suffered intense grief and disorientation. As a therapist I had helped others through their mourning process, and I had thought that I would be better prepared than most. But I was

Excerpted from *A Heart of Wisdom: Making the Jewish Journey from Midlife through the Elder Years* (Jewish Lights), edited by Susan Berrin. **Rachel Josefowitz Siegel** is a retired feminist psychotherapist and a prolific author of professional articles on feminist therapy, aging, and Jewish women.

not prepared for the intensity of my feelings and their unpredictability. Waves of sorrow would emerge so forcefully that tears were nearly uncontrollable.

Going to *shul* without Ben was agony. His absence overshadowed whatever comfort I might have gained from the liturgy or from the presence of friends and community. Having attended *shul* together for forty-six years, we found that it had become a shared and intimate experience as much as a personal and communal one.

I wished sometimes to shriek and wail as my grandmother might have done, in the manner of some Old World widows only one or two generations removed from the white middle-class norms of North American Jews. *Shul* was a little easier when I attended with a friend or on the rare occasions when my daughter or one of my sons was in town.

Saying *kaddish*, the mourner's prayer, was acutely uncomfortable. Perhaps standing alone in my grief was so overwhelmingly emotional that I needed to protect myself from feeling anything at all. I remember one Friday night service at the National Women's Studies Conference when the women surrounded me and supported me as I wept through *kaddish*. I felt such relief.

Standing alone while saying *kaddish* felt like a metaphor for my entire life. I stood alone in my grief. Now, I stand alone when I rejoice and when I mourn, when I plan and when I worry, when I wake up and when I go to sleep. Alone, I now take care of the many tasks previously done by Ben.

No matter how close I may be to my friends and family, or how engaging my work is, there is always that moment when the work is done, the party is over, and I go home to an empty house and an empty bed. So many times I miss the companionship of going over the day's events together. No one else loves our children and grandchildren in quite the same way, no one else has the same history of interpreting the intricacies and contradictions of our extended family, or understands the in-jokes and the shared opinions. When I return from funerals, family gatherings, and celebrations, I especially feel Ben's absence....

In our family, Passover has always drawn us together more than any other holiday. Ours was a conservatively observant Jewish home that was, in many ways, egalitarian. In the last years of Ben's life, I wanted the seder to be more inclusive of women and less rigorous in kashrut, while Ben wanted to maintain a strictly kosher household. We compromised by simplifying the

Passover preparations without giving up on kashrut, and we feminized the seder without giving up on tradition.

The seder has continued to express some of the most beautiful aspects of our life as a Jewish family. It has also embodied some unresolved tensions around tradition and feminism. Each year since Ben's death as Passover approaches, the question of who will lead the seder occupies my mind and soul.

My children are in their late forties, with their own homes in distant cities. Ben died about three weeks before Pesach, but we still held the family seder in our home that year. The children had made it clear that they would agree with whatever decision I made. Their loving accommodations to my needs—while they too were grieving—meant much to me and brought us closer.

After much thought about who would lead the seder, I proposed that all the children and I share the honor and responsibility. As Charles, Hyam, and Ruth each led a portion of the Haggadah with confidence and *kavannah*, spiritual intention, I was deeply aware that the promise that Ben and I had made under the chuppah, the marriage canopy, to build a Jewish home together had, indeed, been fulfilled.

It was a good seder. The grandchildren made their own contributions. The shared ritual, in the midst of mourning, seemed to bring out the best in each of us. It had always been Ben's seder, and I felt the legacy of his Jewish commitment as our three generations continued on without him. In subsequent years, we have varied the arrangements, but each year I face the same question: Who will lead the seder? I am building the courage to do it myself. But to do this, I would have to make time to study. Leading pieces of the service is not the same as leading it in its entirety. I can hardly imagine how I could sit at the head of the table being totally focused on the Haggadah, while part of my mind is still on the soup and *kneidlach*. There is also the dilemma of being a feminist mother of Jewish sons: on one hand, being deeply committed to egalitarian celebrations; on the other hand, hesitant to usurp the age-old privilege from my sons.

I suspect that underlying these issues is my own struggle with traditions designed to keep a Jewish woman in the kitchen and behind the *mechitzah*, the partition. How can I presume that a woman can lead the seder when not even one daughter is mentioned among the four questioning sons? An inner voice calls this arrogant and competitive. Who am I to challenge the ancient traditions? When Ben was alive, I started to include the stories and voices of women in the seder, but I did this with his support. Now that I stand alone, can I make further changes on my own? Can I fully take charge as I have in other areas of my life? And if not now, when?

The Ultimate Call

Dr. Norman J. Cohen

This is the fast I desire: to unlock the fetters of wickedness, and untie the cords of the yoke, to let the oppressed go free; to break off the yoke. It is to share your bread with the hungry, and to take the wretched poor into your house; when you see the naked, to clothe him, and not to ignore your own kin. Then shall your light burst through like the dawn and your healing spring up quickly; your righteousness shall march before you, the Presence of the Lord shall be your rear guard. Then, when you call, the Lord will answer; when you cry, [God] will say: "Here I am."

Isaiah 58:6–9

It is often easier to hear and respond to the faceless needy, people whom we will never meet, rather than reaching out to our parents, children, spouses, siblings, and partners, since our relationships can carry so much baggage. Their needs are camouflaged by layers of shared experiences and defensiveness.

But when we hear their calls and act righteously, we experience a sense of reward and fulfillment in our lives. When we truly give of ourselves to others, when our goodness is evident, we experience God's presence in our lives. Isaiah asserts: "[When] your righteousness shall march before you, the Presence of the Lord shall be your rear guard."

Excerpted from *Hineini in Our Lives: Learning How to Respond to Others through Fourteen Biblical Texts and Personal Stories* (Jewish Lights) by **Dr. Norman J. Cohen**, a rabbi, professor of midrash, and former provost of Hebrew Union College–Jewish Institute of Religion. Dr. Cohen's other books include *Self, Struggle and Change: Family Conflict Stories in Genesis and Their Healing Insights for Our Lives* (also Jewish Lights).

We are told by the prophet that God does not even notice Israel's fasts, though the people are eager to draw near to the Divine. God demands that the prophet call out (*k'ra*) to them, declaring their transgressions, even in the face of their ritual supplications. However, God will indeed recognize their fasts when and only when these ritual acts are accompanied by deeds of righteousness directed toward other human beings.[1] It is then that they will call out to God (*tikra*) and God will not only hear their prayers, but will respond to them—when God will say, "*Hineini.*"

We, too, will only sense the presence of the others in our lives—whether that be God or others whom we love—when we are truly there for them, when our actions show our deep concern for them. It is only when we respond to them in the fullness of our beings that they will help us grow and find fulfillment.

God will respond to Israel with *hineini*, indicating that the Divine Presence will ensure their survival, as well as their prosperity. According to Isaiah, if they live righteous lives, their "light will burst forth," which is understood by some of the classical commentators as indicating that they will find meaning and success.[2] Their well-being depends on how they treat other human beings, which in turn will affect their relationship with the Divine and God's presence in their lives. When they respond to the needs of others, their needs will be fulfilled by the Divine.[3]

The commentators emphasize that their ability to sacrifice for others, especially those who are oppressed and needy, will eventually lead to their own salvation. Ultimately, God will respond to their call by saying, "*Hineini*" (I am here for you and will redeem you).[4] Just as God promised Moses at the burning bush, "Since you have taken the pains to search for Me, to see My Presence, I, therefore, will reveal Myself to you and redeem your people [from Egypt]," so, too, will God answer and redeem the Israelites in Isaiah's day.[5] According to the prophet, their righteousness will ensure their return from exile. Isaiah said, "Your righteousness shall march before you." God will bring Israel healing, and the people shall once again experience the fullness of the covenant as they live in the Land of Israel.[6]

As it was with Isaiah's contemporaries, so it can be for us. Like them, we are immersed in our own darkness.... We, too, know hopelessness that can overwhelm and suffocate us. Yet, Isaiah reaches across the generations, calling out to us like the blast of a ram's horn, signaling to us that not only can we survive, but we can even flourish once again. If only we can set aside our selfish concerns and sacrifice for others, we can move beyond our own pain and then experience healing and wholeness. We will see the light burst forth like the dawn, as it breaks through the darkness of our own lives.

Recovering Wonder

Rabbi Edward Feinstein

The tiny European gentleman, with a long mane of gray hair, a pointy gray beard, and giant black eyeglasses, would stare out, for some moments, from the rostrum of a university lecture hall, the pulpit of a great metropolitan church, or the bimah of a crowded synagogue, and then he would whisper, "Ladies and gentlemen, a great miracle just took place."

The crowd was immediately silent, arrested by this announcement, and wondering collectively what miracle could have occurred that every one of them had missed?

"A great miracle just occurred," the speaker continued, "the sun just went down."

The crowd never knew how to respond. Some smiled with amusement at this strange prophet. Some chuckled. Some sat up in curious attention.

And then the speaker proceeded to describe how a religious person sees the world. Knowledge, he explained, comes in many forms. It depends on what we wish to know. If you wish to understand the workings of the body, ask a physician. If you wish to understand love, ask a poet. Don't confuse the two. If you wish to cure heart disease, the physician has guidance to offer; the poet will lead you astray. But if you're trying to heal human loneliness, the poet can guide you; the physician can only prescribe sedatives. Religion, he declared, is a way of knowing. It is a way of answering a certain set of human questions. Our problem is that we have forgotten the questions that religion came to answer, just as we have forgotten to stop and notice the wonder of the evening's sunset.

This was how Abraham Joshua Heschel began his public lectures.... Science, Heschel argues, is useful for knowing certain things about our world,

Excerpted from *The Chutzpah Imperative: Empowering Today's Jews for a Life That Matters* (Jewish Lights) by **Rabbi Edward Feinstein**, senior rabbi at Valley Beth Shalom in Encino, California, and lecturer at American Jewish University. Rabbi Feinstein's other books include *Tough Questions Jews Ask: A Young Adult's Guide to Building a Jewish Life* (also Jewish Lights).

but science cannot reach the most important human questions. Science, for example, cannot answer the scientist's own reflective questions: Why do I do science? What are the ethical uses of scientific knowledge? For questions like these, we use a different kind of knowing. This kind of knowing is not scientifically rational, nor can it be gained through dispassionate detachment. It is intensely personal. There is no safe, objective place we can stand to ask such questions. The questions arise from our own deepest life experience, and the insights we seek will shape every aspect of life.

Heschel calls this kind of knowing our "sense of the ineffable."[1] "Ineffable" means all that cannot be expressed in words. Heschel's philosophical project begins with the task of describing this kind of knowing. Because the subject is beyond words, Heschel employs a peculiar vocabulary in a poetic style of writing. He points, alludes, evokes, and invites us to see our world, including its sunsets, through new eyes.

The sense of the ineffable begins in wonder.

> Wonder, or radical amazement, is the chief characteristic of the religious man's attitude toward history and nature. One attitude is alien to his spirit: taking things for granted, regarding events as a natural course of things. To find an approximate cause of a phenomenon is no answer to his ultimate wonder. He knows that there are laws that regulate the course of natural processes; he is aware of the regularity and pattern of things. However, such knowledge fails to mitigate his sense of perpetual surprise at the fact that there are facts at all.[2]

The sense of the ineffable leads us to powerful life moments that concepts cannot capture and words cannot describe. Experiences of wonder, amazement, mystery, and awe signal these extraordinary moments. These moments humble us. They diminish the sense that we have a complete understanding and control everything in our experience. They overthrow our arrogance and open us to a different kind of knowing. "Higher incomprehension," taught Heschel, is the beginning of wisdom.

> The ultimate insight is the outcome of *moments* when we are stirred beyond words, of instants of wonder, awe, praise, fear, trembling and radical amazement; of awareness of grandeur, of perceptions we can grasp but are unable to convey, of discoveries of the unknown, of moments in which we abandon the pretense of being acquainted

with the world, of *knowledge by inacquaintance*. It is at the climax of such moments that we attain the certainty that life has meaning, that time is more than evanescence, that beyond all being there is someone who cares.[3]

The peak of our sense of the ineffable is an ultimate insight, Heschel teaches. This ultimate insight is not an affirmation. It is neither an assertion of God's existence nor a validation of our own significance. The ultimate insight comes as a question, demanding a response.

> Religion begins with a consciousness that something is asked of us. It is in that tense, eternal asking in which the soul is caught and in which man's answer is elicited.... The more we meditate, the more clearly we realize that the question we ask is a question we are being asked; that *man's question about God is God's question of man*.[4]

Through the lens of the ineffable, the ultimate human question about God's existence is rephrased into the question God first put to Adam in Genesis: "Where are you?" (Genesis 3:9). Our search for the meaning of existence is transposed into God's search for a partner to complete the work of creation. Our need for a sense of significance in the face of mortality is met by God's need for human participation in the divine dream of a world of oneness. The only way to answer is through action. Action, too, becomes a way of knowing.

> A Jew is asked to take a *leap of action* rather than a *leap of thought*.... Through the ecstasy of deeds we learn to be certain of the hereness of God.
>
> It is in *deeds* that man becomes aware of what his life really is.... It is in the employment of his will, not in reflection, that he meets his own self as it is, not as he should like it to be. The heart is revealed in deeds....
>
> To meet God means to come upon an inner certainty of God's realness, an awareness of God's will. Such meeting, such presence, we experience in deeds.[5]

The only thing the Bible discloses about God, Heschel observes, is that God cares. "God in the universe is a spirit of concern for life. What is a thing to us is a concern to God."[6] But caring is more than God's. Caring is the quality human beings share with God. It is in acts of caring that the truth of our existence is revealed to us. Caring is a paradox. In performing the selfless act of caring, we come to understand the true nature and capacity of the self. Caring pushes us beyond the boundaries of the defined, narrow self, into a vision of self that includes the other. For Heschel, the act of caring is the answer to the question disclosed by our sense of the ineffable. In caring, we come to experience the meaning of our existence, the significance of our lives. In sharing the tasks of caring with God, we participate in eternity.

Shattered and Whole

Debbie Friedman

Confrontation with death and suffering is part of what motivates us to be. Think about why we do the things we do. Ultimately we are driven by death to live. I do not mean that the fear of death drives us, but death itself, which paradoxically gives us the motivation for an authentic and meaningful life.

I find that I am alone. The fact that no one else in this world will ever *really* know what another feels or fears or wishes or dreams is both exquisite and terrifying. Each of us is unique and alone. Ironically, this is something that we have in common....

When our bodies, the sacks in which our *neshamot* [souls] are housed, begin to give way and we confront death, the psychological walls that we build for our protection also begin to give way. They make way for the soul to emerge, becoming accessible not only for self, but for everybody and everything around. Denial of our finitude would only feed the avoidance of our spiritual potential.

I am reminded of a midrash about the destruction of the Temple. The *Shekhinah* (close-dwelling presence of God, associated with the feminine), which dwelled in the Temple, went out and accompanied the prophets as they warned the people of the potential destruction for which their behavior was paving the way. Each time the prophets were rejected by the people and the *Shekhinah* saw that the people did not change, She withdrew further into the walls of the Temple. Finally, there was nowhere for Her to go. The *Shekhinah* withdrew into the Holy of Holies, the core of the Temple. At that point, the Temple was destroyed.

Excerpted from *Lifecycles*, Volume 2: *Jewish Women on Biblical Themes in Contemporary Life* (Jewish Lights), edited by Rabbi Debra Orenstein and Rabbi Jane Rachel Litman. **Debbie Friedman**, beloved late singer-songwriter, transformed modern Jewish music.

As we build more walls for self-protection, there are fewer places for our souls to emerge. Confrontation with suffering can enable us to lower our walls and provide more space for our souls, but the ultimate liberation happens when we die, and our bodies, like the ancient Temple, turn to dust.

When a disaster befalls us, we have the option to withdraw or to attempt to transform the experience into a teacher for ourselves, our friends, our families, and our communities. Our personal disaster may not only be *our* gift, it may sometimes be another's gift as well. It is our obligation to discover these gifts and give them to others. A word, a thought, a touch may turn someone's life around and give meaning to their existence. And you may never know that you were responsible for that....

I pray that the pain I may experience will continue to teach me so that I may learn to be a source of someone else's comfort. My friends and family have been like angels. I have been enveloped with their gentleness and goodness. I pray that I be granted the physical strength to give as I have been given to, and to participate in the continued healing and well-being of all who touch my life. May I never forget that for every loss we experience, a thousand gifts will come, and the shattered vessels will be ever so slightly more whole than before.

Memory's Price

Rabbi Lawrence Kushner

My father was, among many things, a sign painter. I grew up amidst art gum erasers, mat board, and paintbrushes. So now, every now and then, when I reach out to pick up a roll of masking tape, I bring back more than the tape. Sometimes, for just a moment or two, I cry and I remember how he taught me how to hold a brush.

He was also the first trainer of the Detroit Lions—back in 1935 when they were world champs. Sunday afternoons, while growing up, I would watch their games with him on television. So, even now, when I hear the sportscaster mention the Detroit Lions, without warning, I get sad.

He used to love peaches. They could be in ice cream, or on his cereal, but he especially loved fresh whole peaches. So now, when I drive by a fruit stand selling peaches, every now and then, I imagine that he is with me in the car and how we would pull over and buy a half dozen. And again my eyes moisten.

I have come to regard these unexpected tears as a natural part of the healing process, even as a precious reminder of my love for him. After several years, I am getting used to it, but I hope it never stops.

I feel sometimes almost as if all the things that remind me of my father were joined to me by long, thin, taut wires. And when I chance upon one of those things—the masking tape, the football game, the fresh peaches—one of the wires gets twisted ever so slightly and it pinches out another tear or two I didn't know I had. Even more mysterious to me is that every few weeks, I discover yet another wire. There seem to be thousands of them.

Excerpted from *Invisible Lines of Connection: Sacred Stories of the Ordinary* (Jewish Lights) by **Rabbi Lawrence Kushner**, Emanu-El Scholar at San Francisco's Congregation Emanu-El and adjunct professor of Jewish mysticism and spirituality at Hebrew Union College–Jewish Institute of Religion. Rabbi Kushner's other best-selling books include *God Was in This Place and I, i Did Not Know: Finding Self, Spirituality and Ultimate Meaning* (also Jewish Lights).

When my mother, my brother, and I walked down the aisle just behind the rabbis who were following his casket, I cried openly. The young assistant rabbi looked back in concern to make sure I was all right. I managed to joke, "Six years of psychoanalysis, now I can cry whenever I want."

My father lived to be seventy-six. Not a ripe old age, but long enough to make it to two of the three b'nai mitzvah of my kids. Since he succumbed to a heart attack, neither my brother nor I was able to get there in time, as it says in Genesis, to close his eyes. But we were spared the scene of a hospital room and only have memories of his healthy smile. I suppose I was even fortunate that we had him for eight years after his first big heart attack.

He was my father and he's dead. And every now and then, sometimes once a day, other times every week or two, but sooner or later, one of the wires gets twisted and I cry a little. It is a small price to pay for our love. It is almost as if his death has made his life even more precious.

Acknowledgments

J ewish Lights would not exist without the dedication and inspiration of so many outstanding spiritual leaders who also can write in a way that transforms their ideas into meaningful parts of our lives. We are grateful to all of our authors, and especially to those whose work appears in this collection. They are our rabbis, professors, educators, chaplains, counselors, and community leaders, and they have led us into an era of renewed Jewish spirituality, making Judaism relevant to everyday life.

Likewise, Jewish Lights would not exist without our devoted readers. We are grateful to all of you for supporting our work; for giving our books to your friends, family, and clergy; and for your never-ending exploration of the spiritual life. May this collection be a blessing in your time of grief.

I am also blessed in our work to have outstanding, talented colleagues of many faiths and backgrounds whose spirit and passion they generously and lovingly contribute to our work. Our editorial team is led by Emily Wichland, vice president, whose vision and talent shapes all that we have done for many years. In particular, the idea for this book, and its specific content, resulted from a team effort led by Rachel Shields, project editor, whose editorial skill and personal compassion are reflected throughout. She has been ably supported in this important work by Catherine Woodard, assistant editor. We who benefit from this book express our gratitude to Rachel for making it happen.

As you walk the path from grief to healing, you are not alone. We hope this book is another companion to help you on your way.

Stuart M. Matlins

Notes

Mourning Rituals

1. Stephen Levine, *Who Dies? An Investigation of Conscious Living and Conscious Dying* (New York: Anchor Books, 1982), 85.
2. In addition to Levine, see Elisabeth Kübler-Ross, *On Death and Dying* (New York: Macmillan, 1969); Stanley Keleman, *Living Your Dying* (New York: Random House, 1974); and, in the Jewish realm, Jack Riemer, ed., *Jewish Reflections on Death* (New York: Schocken, 1974).
3. Victor Turner, *The Ritual Process: Structure and Anti-Structure* (Ithaca, N.Y.: Cornell University Press, 1969), 94–130.
4. On correspondence between Jewish mourning ritual and psychological need, see Anne Brener, *Mourning and Mitzvah: A Guided Journal for Walking the Mourner's Path Through Grief to Healing* (Woodstock, Vt.: Jewish Lights, 1993); Audrey Gordon, "The Psychological Wisdom of the Law," in *Jewish Reflections on Death*, ed. Jack Riemer (New York: Schocken, 1987), 95–104; and Mortimer Ostow, "Grief and Mourning," in *The Bond of Life: A Book for Mourners*, ed. Rabbi Jules Harlow (New York: The Rabbinical Assembly), 22–34.
5. Editor's note: These practices are usually only observed in very traditional communities.

How Am I Supposed to Feel?

1. One midrash says that the white spaces between the letters of the Torah are as filled with wisdom as the letters themselves. Our responsibility is to penetrate the wisdom of those spaces to live a life rich with meaning. Each of us must create our own midrashim, and in the process create our lives.

   I believe in the wisdom of those white spaces. I believe in our ability to connect, through those white places, with the source of our healing wisdom. I often begin my workshops or classes by announcing that I am about to introduce the book in which I found the most support for my healing. As the workshop participants poise their pens to write down the title, I hold up a blank book. It is within those blank books that our personal truths are revealed.

What Happens to Us after We Die?

1. Sempo Sugihara was a Japanese ambassador stationed in Lithuania. When the Nazis invaded that country, the Jews were trapped. The Nazis were on one side eager to kill them. On the other side were the Russians, who wouldn't let them in. Russia would open its border and let the Jews in only if they had special visas showing that they were on their way to somewhere else. But no country would give them these visas. Finally, in desperation, the Jews came to Sugihara and begged him for help. Sugihara's superiors in Tokyo told him not to help the Jews, but he ignored that order. He saw the fear in the eyes of

these Jews and he knew that he had to help. Sugihara began writing visas for Jews. With the help of his wife and son, Sugihara wrote 3,500 visas in one night, saving more than ten thousand Jewish lives.

Raul Wallenberg was a diplomat from Sweden assigned to the Swedish embassy in Budapest, Hungary. He was shocked at what the Nazis were doing to Jews. He set up a special zone in Budapest, under the direction of the Red Cross, where Jews were safe from the Nazis. Wallenberg worked tirelessly bringing Jews to safety, sometimes even pulling them off the trains that would have taken them to the concentration camps. By the end of the war, Wallenberg had saved thirty thousand Jews. At the war's end, he disappeared. It is believed that he was arrested by the Soviets and died in a Soviet prison.

Does the Soul Survive?

1. *Pirkei Avot* (Ethics of the Fathers) 4:21.
2. The rabbi who shared this story is Allen Krause of Aliso Viejo, California. I later called his wife, Sherri, to learn more about her experience in the hospital. She shared that with the aid of a psychologist friend she entered into a deep trance to cope with her horrible pain. She became aware in this relaxed state of a blue light passing from her feet and emerging from her head. She found herself feeling peaceful and became aware of a cocoonlike structure around her that served to help her breathe and to turn her. The prayers people said on her behalf formed the translucent cocoon. After her deep trance experience, her treating physician commented that her blood gases had moved from a dangerously low reading to normal. She remained aware of the cocoon around her and the prayers said on her behalf. One particularly difficult night she heard praying in a language she could not discern. Later she learned that a relative by marriage who is Ethiopian had stayed up that entire particular night praying for her in Amharic.

   On the fifth day in the intensive care unit she felt ready to die. She had heard doctors speaking of her low probabilities of healing, but mostly she was wracked with excruciating pain she felt she could not take anymore. Suddenly she felt herself rising out of her body. She knew she was outside because she felt no more pain. Before her she saw a series of doors, some of them opened. She understood them as places and experiences of her life. At the end of the hall she could see a bright light, unlike any light she had ever seen before. It was the brightest of the bright, but it did not hurt her eyes and it seemed to have texture, almost like the fluids of the womb. As she was moving down the hall she felt calm and eager to enter the light. Then she saw a beloved rabbi who had died of a heart condition a few years before. He was sitting on a fire hydrant, as he was often seen doing during his daily walks while alive. He held out his hand and telepathically communicated that she was not to continue toward the light and that she was to go back. Suddenly she was back in her body, once again wracked with pain, but it was a turning point in her recovery.

   Once she recovered, which involved close to two weeks in the intensive care unit, she was a changed person. She had previously identified with the Jewish tradition but was an agnostic about God. After these experiences she felt convinced that there was a God and that prayer actually mattered. She said that she had lost all fear of death. She viewed these experiences as a gift and has since used her experiences to help two people overcome their fear of death, enabling them to die peacefully and with dignity.

Resiliency

1. See "Resilience," Dictionary.com, Random House, Inc., http://dictionary.reference.com/browse/resilience.
2. Ibid.
3. Ibid.
4. Carole Radziwill, *What Remains: A Memoir of Fate, Friendship, and Love* (New York: Scribner, 2005).
5. Douglas L. Carver, "From the Chief," in "Spiritual Resilience: Renewing the Soldier's Mind," special issue, *The Army Chaplaincy* PB-16-09-2 (Summer–Fall 2009): 2.
6. Victor Frankl, *Man's Search for Meaning* (Boston: Beacon Press, 1959), 131.

Responding to Suffering

1. Pema Chödrön, *The Places That Scare You: A Guide to Fearlessness in Difficult Times* (Boston: Shambhala, 2001), 25.

Where Is God When We Feel Alone?

1. The translation that I have employed is from the Jewish Publication Society translation of *The Holy Scriptures* (1917). The JPS has published a more recent translation (*Tanakh*, 1985); but I prefer the older one for its more poetic quality, the majesty of its language, the graphic quality of the images, and the cadence of its verses.

Lingering Grief

1. Bruce Horacek, "A Heurisitc Model of Grieving after High-Grief Deaths," *Death Studies* 19, no. 1 (January 1995): 21–31.
2. Dov Peretz Elkins, ed., *Moments of Transcendence: A Devotional Commentary on the High Holiday Mahzor*, vol. 2, *Yom Kippur* (Princeton, N.J.: Growth Associates, 1990).
3. Ibid.

The Angel of Losses

1. Howard Schwartz, *Tree of Souls: The Mythology of Judaism* (New York: Oxford University Press, 2004), 203–204.

The Echo of Your Promise

1. This poem is based on Psalm 77.

God Is Right Here and Right Now

1. Solomon ibn Gabirol, "The Royal Crown," in *The Selected Religious Poems of Solomon ibn Gabirol*, ed. Israel Zangwill (Philadelphia: Jewish Publication Society of America, 1923), 118. The translation of the Hebrew is mine.
2. This statement is in keeping with Rabbi Leo Baeck. See "Mystery and Commandment," in *Judaism and Christianity* (Philadelphia: Jewish Publication Society of America, 1958).
3. Chaim Stern, *Gates of Prayer for Shabbat and Weekdays: A Gender Sensitive Prayerbook* (New York: Central Conference of American Rabbis, 1994), 87.

Singing in Despair

1. Translated by Simkha K. Weintraub in *Healing of Soul, Healing of Body*, ed. Simkha K. Weintraub (Woodstock, Vt.: Jewish Lights, 1994), 83–89.

How to Become a Blessing

1. For classical sources that make the link between these words, see *Bereshit Rabbah*, Albeck edition [Hebrew], *parashah* 39; and Ramban's *HaEmunah v'Habitakhon, perek* 19.
2. *Sifrei, Deuteronomy, Ekev*. Also see Babylonian Talmud *Sotah* 14a.
3. *The Big Book*, 4th ed. (New York: Alcoholics Anonymous World Services Publishing, 2004), 124.

The Ultimate Call

1. *Targum Yonatan* to Isaiah 58:8 and Radak to Isaiah 58:9.
2. Radak and *Metzudat David* to Isaiah 58:8.
3. *Targum Yonatan* to Isaiah 58:9.
4. See, for example, Hakham, *The Book of Isaiah*, on Isaiah 58:9.
5. See *Midrash Tanhuma ha-Nidpas, Shemot* 15, in this regard, and my remarks in chapter 9, "The Reticence to Respond," in *Hineini in Our Lives* (Woodstock, Vt.: Jewish Lights, 2005).
6. Hakham, *The Book of Isaiah*, on Isaiah 58:8.

Recovering Wonder

1. Abraham Joshua Heschel, *God in Search of Man* (New York: Harper and Row, 1966), 20.
2. Ibid., 45–46.
3. Ibid., 131.
4. Ibid., 162, 132.
5. Ibid., 283.
6. Abraham Joshua Heschel, *Man Is Not Alone* (New York: Harper and Row, 1951), 145.